The
Silent
Guides

BY THE SAME AUTHOR:

The Chimp Paradox: The Mind Management Programme to Help You Achieve Success, Confidence and Happiness

Prof Steve Peters

CREATOR OF THE **CHIMP MANAGEMENT** MIND MODEL

The
Silent
Guides

Understanding and developing
the mind throughout life

Published by Lagom
An imprint of Bonnier Books UK
3.08, The Plaza,
535 Kings Road,
Chelsea Harbour,
London, SW10 0SZ

www.bonnierbooks.co.uk

Trade Paperback 9781788700016
eBook 9781788700436

A CIP catalogue of this book is available from the British Library.

Designed by Envydesign Ltd
Printed and bound in Great Britain by Clays Ltd, Elcograf S.p.A.

3 5 7 9 10 8 6 4

Text © Mindfield Media Limited 2018
Illustrations © Jeff Battista 2018

Professor Steve Peters has asserted his moral right to be identified
as the author of this Work in accordance with the Copyright, Designs
and Patents Act 1988.

The Silent Guides title was chosen to depict the role that unconscious beliefs and coping strategies play in our lives. They can develop into unrecognised habits that are powerful in guiding our behaviours, emotions and thinking. This book addresses the Silent Guides that can be detected, changed or formed.

I would like to thank everyone who has offered suggestions, read passages, commented and generally been very helpful and encouraging while I wrote this book. There are too many people to mention by name, but your input was greatly appreciated. Special thanks go to Andy Varns and Jessica Radburn for their hard work in finding references and giving recommendations; to Hazel Barker, who joined them in reading and re-reading to add invaluable comments; to Jeff Battista, who patiently designed the graphics and brought to life many important points; to Natalie Jerome and the team at Bonnier Books; and finally, to all those professionals who contributed from varying backgrounds.

Contents

Part 1
Setting the Scene

The first part of this book explains why we might want to consider looking at unconscious beliefs, coping strategies and habits, and offers some encouragement to the reader.

Whether you are reading this book for yourself or with a view to gaining ideas on nurturing or managing a child, it might be good to step back before you begin and get yourself into the right frame of mind. Managing yourself, or having the responsibility for nurturing and raising a child, can be challenging. I would like to offer some general encouragement, before looking at research, practical ideas and suggestions that could help.

Introduction

What this book is about

After writing *The Chimp Paradox*, I was humbled by the response from many members of the public requesting further ideas and information on how we can use neuroscience in an accessible way. I have put some ideas forward in this book.

During our childhood, we learn to manage emotions and thinking by developing coping strategies and beliefs. These strategies and beliefs, whether helpful or unhelpful, are frequently stored in our memory and often progress into unconscious habits for life. Habits are therefore not just actions but can also be repeated beliefs. Unhelpful habits that persist into adult life usually bring stress and can be detrimental to our day-to-day functioning, psychological health and relationships. Therefore, the Silent Guides are unconscious beliefs and behaviours turned into habits that guide or automatically act to take us through life. *Most importantly, we can challenge these underlying beliefs, coping strategies and habits to make sure that we have helpful Silent Guides*.

This book has two themes:

- To help adults to consider and understand where some

of their unhealthy or destructive learnt behaviours and beliefs might have come from, and then offer ways to replace them with healthy and constructive behaviours and beliefs

- To offer ideas and support to parents, teachers or carers that could help children to form healthy and constructive habits and prevent unhealthy or destructive habits from developing

Examples of helpful thinking, behaviours and habits:

- Learning to apologise or say sorry effectively
- Being proactive and stopping procrastination
- Developing a positive outlook
- Changing negative emotions into positive emotions
- Seeking appropriate help
- Learning to collaborate
- Getting over mistakes

Examples of unhelpful thinking, behaviour and habits that can be changed:

Many unhelpful habits are not recognised as being habits. Once we recognise them as habits, we can change them. For example:

- Having a negative outlook as a default position (Chapter 5)

- Being overly self-critical and unable to forgive yourself for mistakes (Chapter 6)
- Holding onto guilt and beating yourself up (Chapter 10)
- Not reaching out and asking for help (Chapter 11)
- Fearing failure and unforgiving perfectionism (Chapter 13)
- Living with low self-esteem (Chapter 13)
- Worrying excessively (Chapter 13)
- Overreacting to situations (Chapter 14)
- Generally moaning and complaining (Chapter 16)

> ## *Important point*
> *We can develop helpful habits and prevent unhelpful habits from forming during childhood. We can change old habits or form new habits in our adult life.*

I have written the book around childhood, but the principles that operate are the same for anyone of any age. Here is a simple example of how a childhood principle can relate to any adult. We know from research that children whose parents or teachers are overly critical can undermine a child's development and create self-doubt.[1] In contrast, praising a child for accomplishments, or efforts made, can give the child better self-esteem. This principle could be applied to any adult, not just a child. If you develop the habit of praising yourself for what you have accomplished, or what effort you have made, then your self-esteem can rise. Having a habit of being overly critical of yourself only leads to self-doubt and low self-esteem. Recognising the habit of unhelpful self-criticism, *and changing it*, can alter self-esteem.

For readers who wish to explain to a child the ideas that are covered in this book, I have also written *My Hidden Chimp*, a children's educational book with graphics, exercises and activities.

Encouragement for the reader

Why consider habits?

As a doctor, my role is to promote both physical and psychological health. My specialist area is the working of the mind. The adversities and struggles that we often encounter as we travel through life are not usually as difficult as the internal struggles that go on inside our own minds. I have the privilege of working with people of all ages, including children, to help them to manage these internal struggles. This is a major part of my work.

From time to time, many of us have experienced stressful or painful emotions coming from internal struggles, so anything that can help to take the stress or pain away, or to prevent it, would be welcome. There are many different aspects of the mind that can be addressed and many different ways of addressing them. One feature that very frequently presents itself is an unhelpful or unconstructive habit. When I work with someone and we discover the habits that they operate with, it can make a tremendous difference to their life if they can modify, change or replace the unhelpful ones.

Being a parent, teacher or carer of children

Parents, teachers and carers should find nurturing and interacting with children an amazingly rewarding experience, and in most cases it is. However, the reality is that many adults in this position can also find it very stressful and challenging. So it might be worth first looking at addressing this stress before we embark on the major themes of the book.

It is perfectly normal to experience moments of feeling unable to cope, not knowing if you are doing the right thing, wondering how you are going to manage and, in some cases, wanting to just run away! It might be reassuring to know that most parents are looking for that elusive manual that will help them to become the perfect parent. Sadly, there isn't one. This is because there are so many differing opinions, even among the experts. **The way that you raise your child will come down to you.** This still leaves many parents, teachers and carers concerned about the effects on the child if they are getting it 'wrong'. This can be very unsettling.

There might not be a 'right way' to raise children, but there are some guidelines that can help a child to be happy, confident and well-rounded socially. There is a wealth of research on the topic, and some references are offered in this book if you wish to follow up on the work undertaken so far.

It is never an easy role to nurture, support or educate a child. It can be a steep learning curve. *The most important factor is that the child feels wanted and secure.*

When a child feels insecure with feelings of rejection by parents or peers, some regions of the brain remain underdeveloped.[1] [2] This then affects them later in life and they can show sensitivity towards possible rejection. Any adverse life events during childhood, not just rejection, can affect the development of some areas of the brain and result in poor emotional management later in life. The way this happens is explained in the notes section at the end of this book.[3]

One subtle way of 'rejecting' a child is to not take them seriously. Children, just like adults, like to be listened to and taken seriously. As a doctor, I have patients who can sometimes present a worry that really concerns them. Even if I can see that this is nothing serious, nor anything to worry about, it doesn't help the patient if I don't accept that, to them, it is serious and worrying. By taking their concerns seriously, they feel listened to and respected. The same applies to children. So not listening well to concerns and worries, before addressing them, can give the child a sense of rejection.

Don't neglect yourself!

Before interacting with a child or other adult, it is obviously beneficial to get yourself into a good place first. It is clear that looking after yourself not only helps you, but also helps everyone else around you. However, we often forget this.

One method of settling yourself into a good place is to share your thoughts and feelings with others. I would recommend that, when working with or caring for children, you don't try to go it alone. Whenever possible, try to share what is happening with a partner, family member or friend.

Grandparents can sometimes be a stabilising influence on children and their parents, especially when there is parental conflict.[4] A warm parental relationship from at least one parent can help promote resilience in a child for later in life.[5]

Try to make sure you do the obvious!

- Make time out for yourself when possible – adults use a lot of unconscious energy through using vigilance to keep children safe
- Be at peace with yourself; become your biggest fan and not your worst critic
- When possible, have a change of scenery and mix with others
- Try and exercise, if you have the time and energy!
- Ensure you don't neglect yourself, and form your own 'happiness list' – things that make you happy – and try to implement them

Part 2
Some Basic Neuroscience

The second part of the book covers the structure and functioning of the mind. The science of the brain and mind is explained in simple terms. There are references at the end for those who wish to look into the work at a deeper level. The science is translated into a working model, the Chimp model, for easy access to the mind. This then gives us the opportunity to explore ways of managing behaviours, thinking and emotions. Chapter 1 explains the basics of the Chimp model. Those who know the model could use this as revision or move on to Chapter 2.

Stages of the developing mind are worked through, with ideas on how development can be encouraged. Influencing factors are considered as well as how the mind manages these. Finally, the way in which we interpret the world and our experiences is looked at from a practical standpoint.

Chapter 1

The simplified neuroscience of the mind

To understand something that is complex we often use a model. A model is a simplified version of the principles involved. One model of the mind is to consider it as three operating teams that are trying to work together. One team is you and the other two teams form a machine.

This chapter will look at how this model can be applied.

You | The Machine

- The brain and mind, simplified
- The structure of the mind
- The neuroscience of the mind, simplified
- The Chimp model
- Appreciating the influence of the machine

- Decision-making
- How can we manage the machine?
- The mind of a developing child

The brain and mind, simplified

We can think of the brain as the centre for managing everything in our bodies. It controls many physical functions, such as our heart rate, our appetite, our hormone levels and much more. It also has control of many mental functions, such as how we think, how we behave and the emotions we experience. The *mind* is in charge of these mental functions, and this is the aspect that we are focusing on. Clearly the two aspects, mental and physical, do overlap, but let's keep it simple!

Throughout this book I will simplify the structure of your mind, so that you can understand and manage it.

The structure of the mind

The most important point in this chapter is to appreciate that we have a part of our mind that thinks and acts and can run our lives *without our input*.

I will first describe the structure of the mind in layman's terms and then explain the neuroscience. The mind can be seen as divided into two parts: you and a machine. You and the machine think and interpret your world independently. Sometimes you and the machine see things differently. So it helps if we understand how to work with this machine.

You
Think

Machine
Thinks and
stores memories

You interpret events that you experience and are in charge of your own choices. The machine has its own interpretation of the same events and has its own agenda. Very frequently, you and the machine don't agree! For example, you might want to take life as it comes and not stress or overthink things. The machine, however, is programmed to try to make life do what it wants and typically overthinks and stresses about things.

You   **Machine**

Relaxed   Stressed

Rational   Irrational

Realistic   Unrealistic

If the machine takes over, and it can, then you can experience unwelcome behaviours and thoughts. The problem is that the machine has the power to override your own wishes and plans, if you don't intervene. So effectively, your mind is shared between this machine and yourself.

If we look at the machine more closely, we can see that it has two different parts to it. One part thinks and interprets and the other is a memory store. So we now have a thinking part of the machine, a memory part of the machine, and you. So, effectively, there are three teams operating within your mind: you and the two parts of the machine.

Both you and the thinking part of the machine have the ability to use the memory store. This memory store is very much like a computer, so from now on it will be called 'the Computer'. When you go to act, the Computer offers advice from its stored memory.

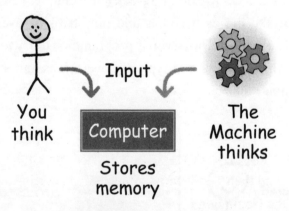

Diana and the roof tiles

Here is an example of this principle in operation. Some strong winds have dislodged a tile on Diana's garage roof. She decides to go up and fix it. When she has climbed on to the roof, her feet slide from under her because the roof tiles are slippery. She falls from the roof and hits the ground but is okay, just very shaken. We all react differently, but this is how Diana stores this information. She puts into her Computer: 'When I go on to some tiles again, I must check to see if they are slippery.' Her machine, which usually overreacts, puts into the Computer: 'Don't ever go onto a roof again, it is dangerous and you will fall.'

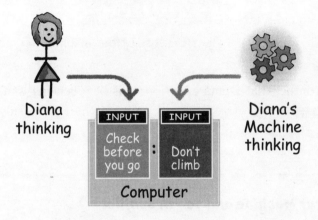

Diana thinking

Diana's Machine thinking

INPUT — Check before you go : INPUT — Don't climb

Computer

When we think and interpret events we usually do this logically and rationally. Our machine cannot do this. It can only think and interpret emotionally and base its logic on these emotions. Therefore, it tends to be catastrophic in its thinking, and then works with feelings when deciding what to store in the Computer.

The problem is, that when Diana next approaches going on to the garage roof, her Computer offers conflicting advice.

The conflict that Diana experiences is between her and her machine.

Your Machine and You in conflict

Take a moment to pause and think of examples where you and your machine have come into conflict. If you find it difficult to think of any examples, here are some suggestions that most of us have experienced as quite frustrating!

You		The Machine
Choosing to act	OR	Putting things off and procrastinating
Keeping perspective and being calm	OR	Not seeing the bigger picture and stressing
Deciding on which healthy food to eat	OR	Grabbing the most pleasurable
Finding a solution to a problem	OR	Focusing on the problem

The neuroscience of the mind, simplified

When we use scanners to watch an image of the mind in action, we see various structures or areas lighting up when they are active. Simply speaking, we can see three different teams in action: you, your thinking Machine and the

Computer. Each of these teams appears to have a team leader. These leaders could be thought of as being represented by the following structures:

	Main structure
You	The dorsolateral prefrontal cortex
Your Thinking Machine	The orbitofrontal cortex (with help from the amygdala)
The Computer	The hippocampal gyrus (also with help from the amygdala)

Simplified brain diagram to show the three team leaders

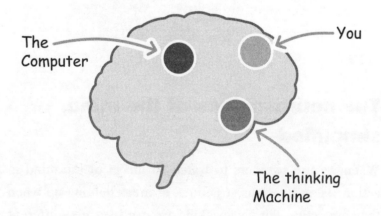

The three leaders call on many other parts of the mind for help. Some parts of the mind can multitask and some parts can be a member of more than one team. For example, the amygdala multitasks by storing emotional memory and also uses flight, fight or freeze to help us to react quickly in a perceived emergency. As the mind is complicated, I am going to keep it simple and assume we have these three teams operating together. By using this model we can make sense of complicated neuroscience. The principles applied are accurate, but simplified.[1]

The Chimp model

The Chimp model[2] is just a model! We don't have a Chimp inside us! The model gives an easy way to access the mind and understand the neuroscience in a simplified way. The thinking part of the machine now becomes known as the 'Chimp'.

Why am I using the terms Human, Chimp and Computer? We could call these three teams in your mind anything we want, but I am giving them the names Human, Chimp and Computer to help us to recognise how they operate.

You | The Machine

The Human

The Human team is where you consciously think and make decisions: so this part is you.

This area interprets any information in a logical and rational way. It uses a *cognitive* approach for understanding. This means it uses *thinking* in a rational way to work out what is happening and how to proceed. It therefore learns by making sense of things. It particularly likes to ask questions. The Human also performs executive skills, such as organisation, prioritisation, ability to focus, ability to remove distractions and many other higher functions.[3] The Human has conscious awareness and is effectively you.

The Chimp

The Chimp team covers the fast-reacting systems within the mind that we have no control over but we can influence.

The Chimp thinks independently of us and can make decisions. Chimpanzees (along with many other creatures) have a similar operating area and when we both use this area, we can at times act in a similar manner! I therefore used the term 'Chimp' to describe those circuits in the brain that can often cause us some problems by hijacking us. These areas interpret any information from an *emotional* basis by using feelings and impressions.[4] [5] The Chimp therefore uses an emotional approach to understanding and learning, and works more with behaviours. It learns by trial and error and works impulsively. It doesn't think things through but *reacts* to situations. This area is very fast to react and *can override the Human*. This part of the mind is there to help us, but sadly it doesn't always help!

The Computer

The Computer team is a memory bank that reminds and advises the Human and Chimp teams of previous experience or knowledge. The Computer also has the ability to follow programmed thinking and behaviours.

The Computer does not interpret, so it is different to the first two teams. When the Human and the Chimp go into action and begin interpreting the world around them, they call on the Computer.[6] The Computer is like an advisor, but one who can also take over and act alone. The Computer is spread all over the brain and represents many aspects of brain functioning, including memory and automatic responses. It is programmable and will also spot patterns and make decisions for us, depending on what pattern it recognises. It therefore forms and stores learnt behaviours and beliefs. The details of the neuroscience of memory are in the notes section at the end of the book.[7][8][9][10]

When we consider habits, we see them as automatic behaviours that have been programmed into the Computer. Two terms that I use a lot when working with the Chimp model are 'Autopilots' and 'Gremlins'. Autopilots are helpful or constructive beliefs or behaviours that are programmed into the Computer. Gremlins are unhelpful or unconstructive beliefs or behaviours programmed into the Computer. So habits are part of these Autopilots and Gremlins. So, for those who know the Chimp model well, what we are doing is finding and replacing Gremlins with Autopilots.

For this book, I will stick to the terms 'helpful' or 'unhelpful habits', to avoid too much terminology.

Appreciating the influence of the machine

Our starting point is to appreciate and understand the strong influence of this internal machine and how it affects the way in which children and adults function.

Clearly, the machine and yourself are one person. For example, your hair colour or your eye colour belong to you, but you don't choose them. The machine belongs to you and is your unique machine, but you haven't chosen it. The machine can therefore drive us to do certain things, such as eat, search for security and find companionship, and it also has the ability to think for us and make decisions. As said earlier, effectively this 'machine' part of the brain is not within your control. Your brain machine has common features shared with everyone else, but your machine is still unique.

So, for example, the eating drive is stronger in some of us than others. The need for security differs from person to person. The machine is programmed to react to your surroundings, keep you safe and ensure that you thrive. It just tends to overreact.

At different stages in your life, the machine will change its method of operating and alter its way of learning. This is a critical point for understanding children and young adults. By understanding how these changes happen, we can help young children and adults to make the most of these stages. Basically, the Human part of the brain matures very slowly, and steadily learns how to manage the Chimp and how to programme the Computer.

Important point
Our mind is constantly developing and maturing, both physically and psychologically.

When we are working with children, if we can distinguish between the child and the machine this will help us to see the child's behaviour in a different light. Just as adults experience unwelcome hijacks and frequent unhelpful interference from the machine, so do children. We feel upset when the machine hijacks us, because we don't agree with what it has done.

The good news is that we can learn to manage this machine and therefore influence it, and even override it. We can make our own decisions and think independently of the machine. A critical point is that we can help children to understand their own machines and we can also help to steer and nurture how a child's machine develops and functions.

Important point

We can help a child to learn about their mind and how to manage it, and we can help to nurture the development of a child's mind.

Decision-making

If we now take a look at the way in which we make decisions using the model, we can see that the first area to act is the Chimp. It acts by making an impulsive emotionally based decision. However, before it acts, it must get advice from the Computer to help it to make a decision.

If the Computer recognises the situation and has a plan to deal with it, then the Computer will take over. For example, let's assume you have to make a decision on what to wear for a job interview. The Chimp makes an impulsive decision based on what it feels would be right and then calls on the Computer to give some advice. The Computer has stored memory and will feed back a lot of ideas and thoughts from past experience.[11] [12] That advice might change the first impulsive decision.

Alternatively, your Computer can just automatically put an appropriate choice of clothes on, without needing you to think.

The Human receives the information later than the Chimp and Computer. If the Chimp and Computer haven't managed to come to a decision, then the Human will help by using a logical approach. The Human also consults the Computer and then decides on what to do. It might agree with the Chimp's decision or it might be in conflict.

The meeting

Often in discussions in meetings, people allow their Chimps to take over and voice opinions first. These opinions are usually fuelled by emotion and evoke further emotional responses in others. After some time, things generally calm down and then the Humans begin to look at facts and use logic for the discussion, which then becomes constructive, and solutions or agreements are worked out. A lot of time and energy could be avoided if the people entering the meetings began in Human mode and represented their Chimps' feelings in a rational and calm manner.

This scenario demonstrates the way in which we naturally operate, if we allow the mind to run its course when making decisions or discussing things. We can, of course, learn to change this pattern by developing a new habit of managing the Chimp before making decisions or discussing things.

However, just to throw things into the air again, sometimes the Chimp's impulsive, intuitive feel is better than our logical approach! This is because sometimes we don't have enough facts, or because our so-called facts are not accurate, whereas our intuition could accurately recognise a pattern that will predict what is going to happen. A problem arises if there is a difference in the final decision between Chimp and Human. Another potential difficulty is that the Chimp always gets information first and acts so fast that the Human might not even get a say.

Simply speaking, there are three possible ways to make a decision:

- Impulsively via the Chimp, with possible advice from the Computer
- Rapidly via the Computer, with programmed automatic responses
- Steadily and rationally via the Human, with possible advice from the Computer

Here are some examples of the Human and Chimp in conflict

Kim and being healthy

Kim understands that being healthy is a good thing. However, even though Kim knows exactly what to do to become healthy, this just doesn't happen. When Kim decides to go for a walk, somehow her mind interferes and forms different plans. When she decides not to become stressed about this, somehow her mind begins to worry and overthinks things.

The question she asks is, 'Why can't I just do what I want to do and have the emotions that I want to have and carry out my plans?'

Jack and his frustration

Jack has just been given some unwelcome news that will affect his plans for the day. He gets frustrated and makes unhelpful comments, and when people try to calm him down, this gets him more agitated. He behaves in a way that he doesn't want to, and later when he either sorts things out or realises it is not the end of the world, he calms down and regrets how he reacted.

If we scanned his head to see what was going on inside it during this time, we would see his Chimp grab more oxygen in his brain and take over against Jack's wishes. His Chimp would not see the bigger picture, ***because it can't***, and it would not think of a rational way to deal with things, because it doesn't work with rationality but rather with emotion.

Maggie and the decision

Maggie has to make a decision between two jobs that are on offer. Her Chimp senses that she might get it 'wrong'. It now hijacks her and begins to worry and overthink everything. Maggie's Chimp paralyses her from making a decision. She knows this is unhelpful and that in the end she will be fine with whichever job she takes, even if it turns out not to have been the best option after all. However, because the Chimp is more powerful, Maggie is stuck.

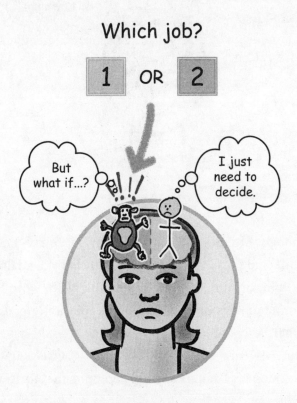

Muhammad and the error

Muhammad was struggling to find an address while driving his car. His Chimp became agitated and caused a lapse in concentration, which caused him to marginally go over the speed limit and the police pulled him in. They issued him with a ticket and he returned home.

Although Muhammad accepts that his error was not deliberate and that it is not the end of the world, he finds his Chimp hijacks him for the next week with worries and agitation about his error. The Chimp constantly goes back over what he could have done and how it could have been different. Muhammad knows that this is not helpful, but he just can't stop his Chimp from not accepting the situation and from worrying.

How can we manage the machine?

This means managing the Chimp and programming the Computer.

We have several options for managing the Chimp:

- Manage the Chimp *before* it hijacks you
- Programme the Computer to advise the Chimp
- Programme the Computer to take over
- Have your own Human plan

Manage the Chimp before *it hijacks you*

Managing the Chimp before it hijacks you means nurturing your Chimp. In other words, looking after your Chimp, emotionally and psychologically. For example, don't allow yourself to be put into a position that could be avoided and which you know could cause your Chimp stress. So, for example, avoid trying to do two things at once: Muhammad could have stopped his car and not allowed his Chimp to

I will be a lot less trouble if you look after me.

become agitated and lose focus by driving and searching at the same time.

Nurturing could also mean things such as having time out, or building your self-esteem or resilience so that the Chimp feels reassured. It can also mean allowing yourself to express your feelings in a constructive way, so that the Chimp can express what it feels. So there are various ways to manage your Chimp.

Programme the Computer to advise the Chimp

The Chimp looks to the Computer before it acts, which takes it less than a split second to do.[13] However, during this split second the Computer has an opportunity to advise and influence the Chimp greatly before it acts. For example, let's say something has annoyed the Chimp and it is about to react. When it looks into the Computer, it finds it is

I need advice

Advice offered

Take a deep breath... and think again.

programmed to tell the Chimp to take a deep breath before speaking. This advice is likely to stop the Chimp from acting impulsively and regretting what it might have said. So from the earlier example, Jack could have programmed his Computer with this advice and it might have helped him to prevent his unwelcome behaviour. Something as simple as taking a deep breath can have great rewards! This simple step can give the Human a chance to speak and bring perspective to the situation.

Programme the Computer to take over

The Computer can act much more quickly than the Chimp and, if it is programmed to act in a given situation, it will take over from the Chimp. For example, we can have a fixed programmed response for any situation that is upsetting us. So we might programme the Computer to say, 'Could you

give me a moment, please?' This simple phrase can prevent us from being pressured into reacting in a way that we might later regret. We could alternatively programme the Computer to learn to distance ourselves from a stressful situation in order to regroup and gain perspective.

Have your own Human plan

In the example of Kim and the walk, she could recognise the Chimp interfering and be firm with it and learn to stick to her own plan and reject the Chimp's ideas and thoughts. *The Chimp is making an offer or suggestion and we can reject this offer.* We can be firm and put our Chimp in its place!

Our Chimps are likely to be quiet and have no need to get involved in situations if they see no danger, threat or excitement. This means the Human (which is you) must now take over with decision-making. Therefore, it is helpful if you have been proactive and formed ideas and plans on how to respond to situations and programmed these into your Computer. Managing your mind effectively means being proactive. You are more likely to function effectively if you have worked out set responses to given situations that you meet frequently. For example, developing a set routine that is efficient when you arrive at work. The Computer will then take over and perform efficiently. These routines can also be programmed for our emotions, such as an emotional response to stress, for example.

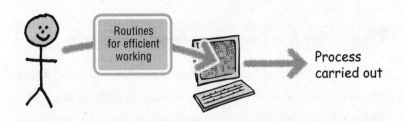

How could Muhammad manage his Chimp, now that it is out?

When the Chimp keeps reacting, it will look to the Computer. So here are some examples of truths that Muhammad could place into his Computer that might settle his Chimp down:

- Everyone makes mistakes and they eventually get sorted out
- There is nothing I can do now but focus on the solution, not the problem
- I can't change the past, but I can choose my reaction to it
- Thankfully no one got hurt and I can learn from this

I am sure you can add some obvious truths of your own to the list. *As long as these facts resonate* with Muhammad then his Chimp will settle down.

The mind of a developing child

Now that we have an understanding of how the adult mind functions, we can look at the mind of a developing child and appreciate the differences in functioning. We will do this in the next chapter, but first an example of how some children used the model and then a summary of the chapter.

The Chimp corner

I wrote *The Chimp Paradox* for adults, and years later I received a scrapbook from a school. The teacher had read the book and explained to the children about their Chimps. The children had composed letters to me, telling me about their Chimps.

I was so impressed and humbled by it that I phoned the school and went to visit them. It was a great experience. The children were about eight years old. I saw that a corner of the classroom had been hived off. When I asked about this, a young boy explained that it was the 'Chimp corner'. He said that if someone becomes a Chimp, they help them to go into the Chimp corner, and they come out when they are Human again. In the Chimp corner they can let their Chimp out. It was amazing to see in action! According to the teacher, the children had come up with the idea themselves. No judgement, no repercussions or assumptions, just acceptance and a practical way to help someone come out of a Chimp hijack. Amazing team-bonding in action!

Summary

- The mind is responsible for our mental functioning
- The mind manages our emotions, thinking and behaviours
- You share your mind with a complex machine
- The machine has two parts: the Chimp and the Computer
- The Chimp thinks and interprets, has its own agenda and can override you
- The Computer advises both the Chimp and the Human, and is programmable by either
- The Chimp always goes first when reacting to situations
- The Chimp's reaction can be modified by advice from the Computer
- If programmed, the Computer can override the Chimp

Chapter 2

The developing mind

This chapter will first use the Chimp model to explain the development of the child's mind, and then in the next chapter we will look at the neuroscience.

- The Chimp hijack
- The mind of the adult and child compared
- How you can help
- The developing mind

The Chimp hijack

One of the catalysts for me to write this book was an incident on the London Underground. Some years ago I was travelling on the Underground, when a group of young schoolchildren boarded with their teacher. The children were about seven years old. They had left one train to change to another. As the train began to pull away, it went in the same direction as the train that they had just got off. One little girl realised this, and her Chimp panicked. She began shouting to the teacher, 'Miss, Miss, we are on the wrong train, we are going in the same direction!' Her Chimp was in quite a state. The teacher, who was clearly under pressure, reacted from her own Chimp and shouted at her: 'Yet again, it's you interfering!' At this point, her classmates immediately began jibing at her and pointing their fingers, 'Yes, it's you again.' The little girl dissolved.

I appreciate that the teacher was under pressure, but I thought it sad that the little girl could so easily start developing a poor self-image as a result of a Chimp hijack. I managed to keep my Chimp from speaking, but thought how life could be so different if we all understood the way that our minds work. If the little girl had been told, 'It's just a Chimp hijack and we all have them', she might have had a very different view of herself and her classmates might have been more supportive.

The mind of the adult and child compared

In the last chapter, we considered how an adult manages their mind. Using the model, we saw three systems in operation: the Human, the Chimp and the Computer.

In an adult:

- The Human is fully mature and fully functioning by around the age of 30 and can programme the Computer. [1] [2]
- The Chimp is still running true to its nature.
- The Computer is programmed with automatic behaviours and strategies to deal with day-to-day life. It also has established values, beliefs and perspective. The Computer can therefore come to the rescue by advising the Human

and Chimp or by taking over and preventing a potential Chimp hijack.

In a child:

- The Human is very immature, undeveloped and struggles to programme the Computer.
- The Chimp is inexperienced, but very active. It is also immature and vulnerable.
- The Computer is usually poorly programmed or not programmed at all, has few constructive strategies and cannot sensibly advise the Human or the Chimp. It also lacks clear values, doesn't know the truths of how the world works and cannot retain perspective.

How you can help

It is clear that, in order to help a child, the adult must effectively become the child's Human. The adult can then help to programme the child's Computer with habits, values, truths and perspective.

Research and science tell us that we can support, guide, encourage and influence the development of the child's mind in several ways. We will look at this in detail under the ten habits that follow.

From a practical point of view, here are some simple reminders of the obvious. Before you interact with a child, it helps if you can:

- Make sure you are in a good place yourself
- Try to remain emotionally stable, consistent and reassuring

- Recognise the difference between the child and the machine, and respond appropriately
- Accept the nature of the child's developmental stage and their possible limitations
- Expect the child to be hijacked by their Chimp and have a constructive thought-through programmed response in *your own* Computer system

The developing mind

During development, the child will go through stages. Here are some examples:

1. The child will experience drives that will change in strength. For example, they will begin with a strong drive for security and to remain with their parent or guardian,[3] but this will be challenged by an independence drive that will gradually take over in their early teens.[4]
2. The child will go through stages of understanding how another person's mind works and how to interact with others.[5] [6]
3. At times, the child will not be able to do certain things, such as use sound judgement or make rational decisions. With time, these skills will develop and, if the parent or guardian can be aware of these stages, they can have realistic expectations of the child.

The Chimp and the Computer develop first

The Chimp begins to develop in the womb as early as eight weeks into foetal life.[7] As it develops, it stores its emotional memory into the Computer, which is also developing.

Emotional memory
being stored

Emotional memory means that we get a feeling about an experience but can't recall facts.[8] [9] For example, if a two-year-old child fell from a climbing frame, they would only store that climbing frames make them feel nervous, but they wouldn't be able to remember why. Animals also store emotional memory and this can affect the way they behave. These memories can be linked inappropriately. For example, I once had a puppy that experienced a fright when a loud gate slammed nearby. By chance, a young child was standing near the gate. From then on, whenever the puppy met a young child it would become frightened. Even as an adult dog, it could not relax near children.

Often, very young children make links by using emotional memories, which are hard to break. It can help to appreciate that if a child appears to be acting irrationally, they might be working from an emotional memory that cannot be recalled.

The Human arrives

It is easiest to think of the Human as being virtually absent for the first three years of life. When the Human does develop, it will store factual memory in the Computer. This is why our first factual memories don't occur until we are around three years old – because effectively we weren't there until then! So our Chimp has a great head start to lay down feelings for situations, without any recall of facts.

As we go through childhood, these two teams of Human and Chimp will try to work together. They will both keep inputting information into the Computer. The Chimp will input emotional memory and the Human will input factual memory. The Human team will steadily have more and more influence as it puts more information into the Computer. It won't just store memory but also beliefs, values and behaviours that are constructive and helpful for day-to-day life.

| Child | Adolescent | Adult |

Your role as the child's Human

So, in terms of the Chimp model, we can think of the child's mind as developing the Chimp first. The Chimp then starts to programme the Computer for a few years, and finally the Human develops. The last part of the brain to develop is the Human and therefore we expect to see a lot of unwelcome Chimp activity in childhood and adolescence.

When adults manage their minds they have several ways in which to do this, whereas the child doesn't. The child doesn't have a Computer that has experience, wisdom or even much awareness of how the world and other people function. Disturbingly, the Chimp will therefore programme the Computer most of the time! This can be even more stressful for the child: they don't have a fully formed or functioning Human and therefore can't make sensible decisions, organise themselves, prioritise, see consequences, programme the Computer or even know what the 'truths of life' are. The list of limitations is extensive!

So, if you imagine a child as having a very powerful unmanaged Chimp, with little input from either Computer or Human, then lots of things might make sense.

Effectively you, the adult, can become their Human and their Computer.

You can't rush the development of the Human within them, but you can help to nurture it. You can assist in areas of the Human development within the child, such as interpersonal skills and awareness. Development of the Human takes time and can continue for 30 years!

The Computer is a different story. You can help develop the child's Computer at any age. This can be done by establishing constructive behaviours or habits and also helping the child to create beliefs based on truths and facts, as you see them.

The Computer works particularly well with behaviours and being programmed.

Important point
Children usually don't welcome their own unhelpful Chimp activity. They just don't understand how to manage it.

Summary

- In adults, the Human, Chimp and Computer have all matured
- In adults, the Human can programme the Computer, which can then manage the Chimp
- In children, the Human is very undeveloped and cannot programme the Computer well, so the Chimp is poorly managed

- In children, the Chimp is very active and programmes the Computer, unless an adult intervenes
- Being in a good place yourself is the best foundation for helping a child
- Learning to distinguish the child from the machine is very helpful for managing the child and your responses to the child and machine.

Chapter 3

The neuroscience of the developing mind

As children grow up, there are a number of factors that influence the development of their minds. These can broadly be categorised as internal and external factors. Understanding them can help in guiding your responses, which will then influence the child's responses.

Influencing factors

- Internal factors
  - Genetic and biological
  - Developmental
- External factors
  - People
  - Environment and culture

Influencing factors

The way in which influencing factors act is obviously complex. To simplify things, which will give us a structure to work with, I will divide the influencing factors into two:

- Internal factors (generally covered by 'nature')
- External factors and how the child interprets these (generally covered by 'nurture')

Major influences on a developing child

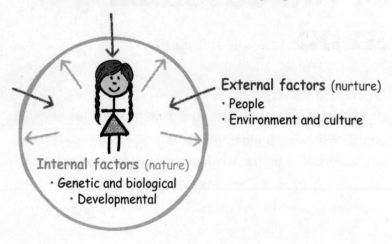

Internal and external factors are obviously not independent of each other and often act together. Every child is unique and each one will be at a different stage of development. As each child is an individual, I will leave it to you to decide where you see the greatest influence on your child.

We can consider a few selected aspects of development and some points that might help in promoting psychological growth.

Internal factors (imposed from within the child)

- Genetic and biological
- Developmental

Genetic and biological factors

Within the womb

We start life as a single cell, with an instruction manual that we inherit from our parents. This instruction manual is called our genes, which tell the body what to do, such as form a liver, produce some hormones or give this person brown hair. However, as these instructions are being followed, they can be influenced by external factors. For example, we know that anxiety traits can be inherited,[1] but we also know that if we work on managing anxiety then the genes either modify their influence or become overruled and a relaxed person appears.[2] [3] We know that, to a large extent, genes determine our 'intelligence' (no matter how we choose to define the term 'intelligence'),[4] but we also know that with suitable nurturing, intelligence can arguably be raised.[5] Genes and their interaction with the environment are both essential for natural development.

The nervous system that helps us to interact and understand our world starts developing in the womb almost immediately. By eight weeks old the sensation of touch has developed[6] [7] [8] and by twelve weeks old the brain has its major structures in place.

At twelve weeks old the foetus is about around three centimetres long.[9] Within the brain, we can see nerve cells being produced that move about in position and form pathways and connections with each other.

It is at this very early stage that personality traits begin to appear. The foetus shows a distinct pattern in response to stimuli, with some foetuses being very responsive while others are not. For example, each foetus shows an individual response to the mother's sleep-wake patterns or to her voice.[10] Research shows that high-activity foetuses show similar temperament scores when the baby is six months old.[11] The important point to reflect on is that our temperament is being formed without any input from us. Our genes are working to form our personality. The mother's influence with sleep patterns and tone of voice is modifying the expression of those genes. The parts of the mind that are mainly developing at this stage are the Chimp circuits, which contain lots of our basic drives and instincts and are developed before we are born. So the body and brain are already prepared for starting life.

Not all of our genes start instructing our bodies in the womb; some will activate at different times during our life. Many stay dormant for years. For example, our sexual preference (who we are attracted to) is formed independent of our gender identity (the sex we feel we are) during the first six months of life and is ready to take influence much later in our life. This sexuality results from an interaction between our genes and the hormones that are being produced.[12] Some forms of depression are driven by our genes and might wait for over two decades before they express their influence.

At this point, depressive illness can appear, despite a person leading a healthy lifestyle.[13]

> ## Important point
> *Our temperament and behaviours have a given biological input from our genes, which we learn to work with, modify or override.*

Infant years and childhood

The very early years of life are built on instincts and drives that help us to survive. Following birth, we have in-built responses to certain stimuli. For example, very young children and very young chimpanzees share an in-built fear of snakes and spiders.[14] [15] The strength of their reaction will vary from child to child, but many will carry this fear of spiders into adulthood, if it is not appropriately overridden by rational thinking.

In-built responses are called instincts and are helpful for protecting us. These are different to learned responses. For example, fearing heights is in-built and protects us, whereas fearing a dog that has bitten us is a learnt response. During childhood there are drives that help the child to stay safe. Drives are in-built and compel us to act. The drive to find food is an obvious one. One of the most important drives is the need for security, which the child will usually get from the parent or caregiver.[16] Even if a parent is abusing a child, the child will still strive to return to them, compelled by this drive for security, fuelled by an attachment to the parent.[17] This situation can leave children open to exploitation, disrespect and abuse.

Role-modelling

We all tend to copy what we see, unless we challenge this with our reasoning. Children learn a lot from watching and copying, and they particularly use role models for learning. This covers not just patterns of behaviour but also values as demonstrated by behaviours.[18] [19] [20] Social support outside the family can produce good role models and the evidence is that these role models can help the child to become more resilient.[21] It is during these early years that the child usually role models on the parent. A sobering thought, which is worth reflecting on!

Important reflection

Are you being the role model that you want to be?

Developmental factors

It takes us until we are about 30 years of age before our brain has finally completed maturing.[22] [23] Some neuroscientists would argue that the brain doesn't stop maturing throughout our entire lives. The brain matures with bursts of learning over a period of 20 years or more.[24]

The last part of the brain to complete maturing, the Human, is concerned with judgement and other executive skills, such as organisation and logical deduction. To function well, nerves are coated with a substance called myelin and it is this that continues to be formed, along with appropriate connections, up until around 30 years of age. It does suggest that we ought to see intelligence as developing over a lifetime and not being fixed in adolescence, when we appear to measure this with exams: a mere snapshot of brain development at that stage!

By six years of age, the brain is 90 per cent of the size of the adult.[25] [26] [27] [28] [29] [30] [31] This young brain has far more connections than it needs and it will cut down on these connections during adolescence, as it experiences which ones work to its advantage. At this stage, the brain shows great plasticity, which is the ability to adapt and change function.

By seven years of age, most children have developed their own style of learning. They have begun to use logical thinking, and be reflective and considerate. The child can make decisions in a basic, rational way via their underdeveloped Human circuits. This means they can problem-solve via their Human, rather than just react to situations via their Chimp. However, before the age of eight, the Human dorsolateral areas of the frontal lobe are significantly underdeveloped.[32] This is demonstrated by a young child's inability to separate fantasy and dreams from reality. Some children up to the age of twelve still believe that 'monsters' exist in their wardrobe or under their bed.[33]

Important point

It is worth reflecting on the fact that the typical child and typical teenager will struggle with, or be unable to perform, some specific mental functions. Probably the most important is their limited ability to foresee the consequences of their actions.

Walking with awareness

An example of a simple function that we develop is the ability to walk while also being aware of those nearby. Many children and adolescents are not spatially aware of others around them and will walk into or in front of others. They might also block someone's path but appear not to be aware of the need to make way. This isn't likely to be purposeful, but is a good indicator that the system for awareness and consequences is not fully operational, and has to be learnt as the brain matures and will naturally be acquired with time. (Of course, there are those who never quite get there and some who learn very young!) The implication is that an adult getting frustrated with a child whose brain can't yet do this simple function might look to themselves *to see if their expectation of the child is reasonable*.

Important point

A child might not be able to do what appears to be a simple thing, both physically and mentally, because they have not developed enough.

The influence of genes

The whole point of considering the science and neuroscience behind child development is to understand that often the child is acting under the influence of their genes or on in-built responses. Also, that the mind is maturing and might not be able to perform in the way that the child would like it to. This means that the child might not agree with what they are doing or feeling. Therefore, if we can acknowledge this, we can join forces with the child and help them to understand and manage this situation.

External factors (imposed from outside the child)

Of the many external factors, I have chosen probably the two most significant factors that influence child development:

- People
- Environment and culture

People

Many years ago, John Bowlby[34] [35] reviewed the importance of the relationships that a child has with adults who are close to them. He looked at the way in which children bond to adults and suggested it was based on a need for security. He called his work 'attachment theory'. In essence, he proposed that children need someone that they can run to for security and that this security is based on both a psychological and a physical input from the adult. Of particular interest was the type of attachments that children formed. He gave these various names: secure, anxious-avoidant, anxious-resistant and disorganised.

Secure attachments are the ideal relationships based on trust. The other three attachments describe the child's attitude towards the caregiver: indifference; fear and anger; and a variable response. His work set the foundation for many other theories and studies, virtually all of which suggest the most important factor for a healthy relationship is the presence of a warm and caring reliable adult.[36] If the child has more than one adult with whom it has an emotionally stable relationship, there is evidence that the child will become more emotionally stable. The role of a grandparent can be critical if the parents are unable to provide the stability.[37] In situations of divorce, the child will do better when the parents are cooperative and less well when the parents are hostile towards each other.[38]

One of the key roles that the reliable, emotionally warm caregiver will play is in emotional regulation. This means the caring adult will support and guide the child with their emotional responses in different situations. As the child gains independence, the child will then emotionally regulate themselves. The child usually models their emotional regulation by observing the adults around them, by the home environment and the reaction of the caregiver to the child's emotion. [39]

Without this early stability, and in cases of deprivation, there is evidence of significant problems for the child later in life, such as clinging behaviour, aggression or an increased risk of depression. [40]

Important reflection

How important is it for you to be in a good place if you want your child to do well?

Environment and culture

It's worth thinking about the environment and the cultural values that we present to children. There is ample research to show that a stimulating environment can help a child to progress intellectually and physically.[41] Long-term research shows that a stimulating environment for young children at four years old will enhance brain development. This enhancement is demonstrated when they reach their teens with improved language and thinking ability. It appears that there is a window of opportunity at around four years of age, where the brain shows accelerated development, but less so at an older age of around eight.[42]

A stimulating environment means that the child will explore and develop various skills. Activities, challenges, learning to play a musical instrument, reading and learning by discovery are all considered to be aspects of a stimulating environment. Most children will naturally have stimulating environments and make the most of these, so be careful not to go overboard. There is a difference between stimulation and enforced engagement!

It is only in cases of marked deprivation that research shows evidence of reduced intelligence.[43] [44] [45] There is little evidence that artistic, intellectual or athletic skills have an optimum age for engagement in a child's development. However, there is evidence that it could be damaging to a child to be pressured into these activities too early or in an overwhelming way, when the child is not ready for them.[46]

Our environment is also shaped by culture. The culture we have is based heavily on morals and moral reasoning. As children mature they go through stages of developing moral reasoning. It is worth considering these stages in order to relate to the child's way of thinking and to help to establish a moral basis for life.

Moral reasoning and development

During childhood, moral reasoning shifts from a parental basis to a cultural basis, before moving to an individual basis. Families develop their own culture aside from a society culture and this can have a large influence on a child's perception of right and wrong.

Lawrence Kohlberg[47] proposed three levels of moral reasoning:

- Children begin with reasoning based on rewards and punishments
- Later in childhood, and in early adolescence, reasoning and morals are based on society's rules
- Finally, the adult sees society's rules as only relative, and forms their own morals

During the first stage of moral reasoning, children are often heard telling other children, who they think have done wrong, that they will be caught and punished. Young children also work heavily on the principle of gaining approval by doing the right thing.

During the second stage of reasoning, young adolescents hold discussions about not breaking the law. When someone breaks the law, the young adolescent is quick to condemn and punish the individual.

Finally, when older adolescents and adults consider where

an individual might have broken the law, they tend to think more about the details and circumstances before they reach a moral decision about the person.

Adults can help children by recognising the shift in moral reasoning and promoting discussions around culture that is appropriate to the level of development the child has reached. So, speaking to a young child about rewards and punishments will help them to understand moral reasoning. As the child matures, they will relate more to society's rules and culture. Finally, with an older adolescent, working with shades of grey and considering all aspects of a misdemeanour will help to nurture and mature moral reasoning.

Summary

- Our personality has a genetic component
- Our experiences will modify our genetic input
- The developing mind has some mental limitations
- Reliable, stable, emotionally warm adults are the best basis for a child's emotional development
- A stimulating environment for very young children helps brain functioning later in life
- Moral reasoning develops in stages and each one can be worked with

Chapter 4

How we make sense of experiences

The older we get, the more experiences we accumulate, and the more information we can programme into our Computer. Children, however, have little experience of their world, and so need to be guided by their parents or caregivers in order to make sense of, and to navigate, the world.

- Behavioural learning
- The neuroscience of programming the Computer
- Cognitive learning
- Tidying up the Computer
- Dynamic learning

How does a child make sense of and use experiences?

There are three important ways that a child can make sense of and use experiences to learn from:

- Behavioural
- Cognitive
- Dynamic

These three approaches are not independent but merge together. I have separated them for convenience of understanding. Everybody uses all three approaches every day. Each approach has its merits and potential drawbacks.

Behavioural learning

Behavioural learning involves a three-step process. We experience a stimulus, we respond to that stimulus and then we either repeat the response or try an alternative way of responding.

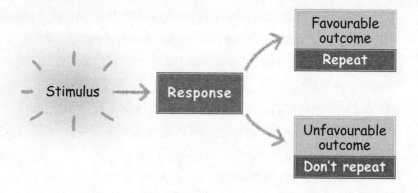

Here are some simplified examples:

Being punished: If a child is caught stealing a biscuit from a tin and is punished, then the child is likely to either *not repeat the behaviour* or *avoid being caught*.

Evidence suggests that the most likely future response to punishment is to ***avoid being caught***![1] Avoidance of being caught leads to possible deceit and lies. One way round this problem is to discuss with the child what they can do if they get tempted to take another biscuit. In other words give them a plan to follow. That plan could be as simple as 'come and talk to me for some praise and some self-praise'.

Positive encouragement and praise work better than punishment, especially for challenging behaviours.[2]

Being praised: For example, if a child, trying to read out loud a passage from a book fails to do this but then gets highly praised for trying, the child is likely to try and read again. This is because the child sees the praise as successful and therefore worth repeating.

A caution

Giving rewards to children can encourage the child to either look for an external or an internal reward. For example, if they succeed in doing something, you can reward them by giving them extra pocket money or a toy. These are external rewards that the child will look for. However, you could also reward them by helping them to feel good about themselves or teaching them how to recognise that what they have done is good in their own eyes. These rewards are internal to the child. There is evidence to show that by giving external rewards, children will look much less to themselves to be driven to do things, whereas giving positive feedback and encouraging children to make choices about their own behaviour will lead to a child being self-driven.[3] Despite research that supports this finding, there is still some evidence that giving material rewards can be helpful.[4]

A really important point
The way that you reward a child can affect the way they approach life.

Variable success

Research shows that, if we sometimes get what we want, but not every time, then we are more likely to keep on trying.[5] [6] This occasional success seems to be addictive to us. For example, occasional small wins on a lottery mean that many people will keep trying for the jackpot, even though it is unlikely to happen, because they have experienced the occasional win.

If, as adults, we are inconsistent with a child and the child gets a favourable outcome only some of the time, then this will strongly encourage the child to repeat the behaviour. This is because they will believe that if they keep on trying then they might get what they want.

Here are some examples:

Going to bed: If a parent insists bedtime is at eight o'clock but then relents occasionally, after pleas from the child, then it is likely that the child will continue to plead, believing and experiencing that the parent could change their mind.

Eating sweets before a meal: If a parent gives way and allows a child to eat sweets just before a meal, then the child is very likely to ask to eat sweets every time and to complain when they don't get what they want.

Reflection point

Consider your own actions when interacting with a child. Are you being consistent with your own responses? Are you promoting the best response from the child?

Problem-creating and problem-solving using a behavioural approach

Developing an unhelpful behavioural pattern to a stimulus can create many problems. First, **we need to recognise an unhelpful response** before it can be changed. The principle is always the same: look for a stimulus and a response. If the response to the stimulus is unhelpful, try to create an alternative response that is helpful.

Here are some examples:

When something goes wrong!

The usual response when something doesn't go according to plan is to moan, complain or become frustrated. This might be very natural, but it isn't helpful. We can programme ourselves to learn to respond to any setback in a constructive way. So a more helpful response to a setback could be an immediate 'this is a moment of opportunity for me'.

For example, the opportunity could be seen as:

- A challenge to learn problem-solving
- A chance to demonstrate patience
- A moment to gain perspective

With some thought, you could find a response that will resonate with your child and yourself. This then becomes a constructive and helpful habit when applied to any setback.

Tidying up a bedroom

The response here will all depend on the age of the child or adolescent! A very common problem for children and adults of all ages is tidying up after themselves. I will cover this scenario in greater detail in Chapter 16, but the main point of this example in this chapter is for you to consider if your response to the untidy bedroom will evoke the required response from the child. In other words, are you helping them to respond in a constructive way?

Typical responses from an adult to a child who has an untidy bedroom are to:

- Offer empty threats
- Complain loudly
- Appeal to the child's sense of respect
- Repeat 'not in my house'
- Condemn using words such as 'lazy'

If one of these were your response, how would you expect the child to feel and respond? The child generally doesn't want an untidy bedroom and certainly doesn't want to feel bad about it. What the child needs is to be empowered and given some direction or guidance. Some alternative possible responses from the adult could be:

- Offer understanding and encouragement
- Make a game of tidying up, with a given short time limit
- Explain how it will make you feel if you see it tidy
- Explain how it will make them feel when it is tidy

If you prefer to go down a different route, then consequences are an option. Consequences are different to punishment, because they are avoidable and occur as a result of the child's own actions or inactions, whereas a punishment is an imposition by an authority figure. So you could explain that an untidy room will have consequences, such as the withholding of privileges until the bedroom is tidy. (Privileges could be time on a computer, watching television or playing outside.)

The neuroscience of programming the Computer

In behavioural therapy, neuroscientifically, the Computer is being programmed with an experience (stimulus) and an expected outcome (response). The Computer will then either advise the Chimp and Human with this experience, or it will automatically take over and repeat a behaviour that it thinks will get the best outcome. When we establish a behaviour, myelin, the insulating substance mentioned earlier, coats the nerves. The more we repeat a behaviour, the more myelin coats the nerves. These myelin-covered pathways become very fast-acting and turn into habits. Therefore, learnt behaviours are strongly reinforced and become hard habits to break, whether they are constructive or not.

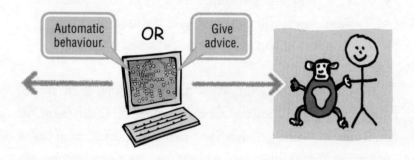

Cognitive learning

When we learn cognitively we learn by thinking, reasoning and forming beliefs. Cognitions are thoughts. The Chimp tends to work in a behavioural way and the Human tends to work in a cognitive way. Cognitive learning means that we think things through and make rational deductions on why something happens and how we can change this if we need to. A cognitive approach also means we can learn from experiences by reflecting on them. When we reflect, we form beliefs and then store these in the Computer. We have already seen that the Human areas of the mind are quite underdeveloped during childhood. However, they still function, and a child can learn to work with the Human aspect of the mind. Therefore, promoting reasoning can help develop it.

Here are some examples of how cognitions work.

Deducing: If a child experiences an adult shouting at them for something that they didn't do, they could form any number of beliefs and then store these in their Computer. For example, they could form beliefs such as:

- There is no point in talking to adults because they don't listen
- Shouting is an adult thing to do
- Children are not listened to

However, they could also form more rational beliefs, such as:

- This particular adult doesn't listen very well
- Life is not always fair
- Sometimes adults can get things wrong

Reasoning: If a child feeds a pet cat and the cat shows affection towards them, they might reason in very different ways. For example, they might reason:

- If you want affection from an animal, then you need to feed it

- If you share your food or sweets with others, then they will like you
- If I have food, then I can use this to please others

However, the child could also reason as follows:

- If I have food, I can control others
- If I have food, I can use this to bargain with
- Offering food is one way to become popular

As can be seen from the two examples, most things we do tend to be interpreted and prompt conclusions. Sometimes these conclusions will be sound and sometimes they won't be. The problem is, that if we put unhelpful or irrational beliefs into the Computer, then this is the advice the Chimp and Human will receive from the Computer at a later time.

Tidying up the Computer

Each child will be putting beliefs into their Computer all day, every day. Many beliefs will be put in without their awareness. Therefore, when we work with children, it's very helpful to keep discussing deductions, reasoning and beliefs with them. This way, we can help to put helpful beliefs and reasoning into the Computer, which will then act as a reference for all decisions made by the Human and the Chimp. The importance of the Computer for all of us can't be overemphasised. It holds the power to advise on decisions in all areas of our lives.

When working with children, behavioural and cognitive methods go together as they are intrinsically linked. So, when developing behaviours, it is very helpful to explain and reason with a child in order to strengthen and back up the behaviours with rational thinking.

Important point
Discussing beliefs and reasoning is a very powerful way to help children to establish constructive habits.

Dynamic learning

Dynamic learning is not an easy concept, so I will try to simplify it. Freud[7] first postulated the idea that a lot of what happens in our heads is unconscious, and many other therapists followed with more ideas on how this might work. We can consider dynamic learning as consisting of three main themes:

- Drives
- Transfer of emotions
- Defensive thinking

Drives

Drives are forces that compel us to act in order that we can survive. So, for example, we have an eating drive. This drive gives us hunger and we then stop the drive from acting by eating. We have a drive for security and once we feel secure we relax and the drive goes away. Security is a major drive in children and is usually satisfied by a parent or equivalent.

The drive for security is important to recognise because if a child feels insecure then it is very likely to act in some way to resolve the drive. The actions it takes might not be appropriate or be misread.

Babies and very young children usually go through a period of development when they become very wary of strangers.[8] [9] They might repeat this at different ages during childhood. This is a natural response that is helpful to ensure the child stays with those it can trust. During this period the child needs reassurance and time to pass through the phase in a constructive way.

We can help by not trying to change their reaction, but by allowing the child to listen to their feelings and then adding a reassurance and offering a way to manage them. Simply explaining that when they feel concerned they can turn to you could help them.

The drive to make the child feel secure is present in order for the vulnerable child to seek support and reassurance from a parent figure. The first day at school can create a sense of panic and fear in some children. The separation anxiety of losing the parent's protection is in-built in order for the child to seek out the parent. Seeing a distressed child, it is important to appreciate that the child is under the influence of an incredibly powerful drive. Reassurances to the child that it is natural to feel this way might help. Even very young children can understand this if we take time to explain what is happening. It might not stop the feelings the child is having, but it might help them to remove any guilt or sense that they are responsible for the feelings. There is, of course, the argument that we shouldn't be putting children through a separation anxiety situation until they are emotionally mature enough to handle it. The time that a child reaches this stage of emotional maturity will be different for each child.

Children who therefore seem particularly anxious might be struggling to satisfy the drive for security, and reassurance rather than criticism would help.

It is always a difficult decision to make as to whether to encourage a child or to allow them to stand back when trying something they seem unsure of. I mention drives just as a reminder to consider them when trying to understand why a child might be acting in an apparently unhelpful way.

Transfer of emotions

When we experience an emotional event we can store this emotion in the Computer, and it can then be transferred into another situation. These situations can involve people or events.

For example, it is not unusual for children to transfer the feelings they have for a parent towards a teacher. The transfer of these emotions could be towards any authority figure. The transfer will then prompt the child to act in a similar way towards the authority figure as they would as if the authority figure were a parent. Transferred emotions can be appropriate or inappropriate, but they can help to explain some behaviours, beliefs or feelings that a child might exhibit. Adults can also operate in this way.

Emotions can be displaced from one situation to another, which could make it difficult to understand what is in the mind of the child. For example, if a child has not got its own way or has experienced a setback, they could displace any anger or frustration towards another sibling or to a parent. Recognising when a transfer of emotion might be taking place can help parents or caregivers not to personalise any experiences of rejection or hostility from the child.

Teacher

Defensive thinking

This is really about the mind trying to make up explanations that stop us from feeling emotionally stressed. We then believe these explanations. Children demonstrate a number of specific ways of thinking, in order to protect their emotions. For example, if a young child has done something wrong or has seen something they don't like, they can then use what is called 'magical undoing' to protect themselves from emotional harm. This is when the child simply believes that, if they don't believe something happened, it couldn't have happened. For example, if the child hit their younger sibling and was challenged about this, to prevent any feelings of guilt they might magically undo the assault and claim it didn't happen. This is different from lying, because when a child lies they know they are lying, whereas with magical undoing the child truly believes it didn't happen.

Sadly, some adults still operate with this very narcissistic thinking and believe that whatever they think is the truth must be the truth, despite all evidence to the contrary.

Round-up of learning

We have considered three ways in which children can make sense of their experiences and then store information from this learning in their Computer for future reference. Behavioural learning is the chosen method by the Chimp. Cognitive learning is the preferred method for the Human. Dynamic learning is a mixture of input from the Chimp, the Human and the Computer. The Computer uses pattern recognition to predict outcomes.

All of us use different ways of learning and different

methods. There are many styles of learning. For example, some of us prefer visual methods and some prefer practical methods. Individual children need individual approaches. Differences in temperament and learning styles mean that children respond to the same methods with different results. When it comes to helping children and adults to learn, we have to deduce what works best for them. We are all unique.

Summary

- Behavioural learning involves a stimulus, a response and reinforcement
- How an adult responds to a child's behaviour will influence the child's response
- Cognitive learning means learning by thinking, reasoning and forming beliefs
- Children can learn cognitively by discussion and this promotes the use of the Human part of the mind
- Dynamic learning involves managing very powerful drives, transferring emotions and defending against emotional stress

Part 3

Ten Habits and Related Themes

The third part of the book explores ten habits and many related themes that are all shown to give advantage to individuals, teams and relationships in general, and contains many practical suggestions and ideas.

I have chosen ten habits that research has shown give advantages to those who operate with them. As elsewhere in the book, the neuroscience that underpins habit formation is explained in simple terms, and for those interested in further reading, references are included.

These advantages include success factors, improved interpersonal skills, improved relationships and personal well-being. There are, of course, many other desirable habits or behaviours that could have been included. The chapters contain information, ideas and suggestions for you to interpret and consider. Many examples are drawn from the experience of others and what they have found helpful, and I am grateful to parents, teachers and other professionals for their guidance and contributions. ***Only you can decide what works best for you***. I hope that there will be some ideas and suggestions that resonate with you and encourage you to develop new habits or change unhelpful ones.

Each habit is covered with simple scientific information to help appreciate the basis from which it works. When the brain performs a habit, it doesn't rely on thinking, decision-making or memory – it works automatically.

The neuroscience behind habit formation is well researched. Most research points towards habit formation being centred in the basal ganglia and brainstem.[1] [2] Experts differ in their opinions on how long it takes to establish a new habit, but most agree that it takes between three and ten weeks, after lots of practice.[3] [4] [5]

Once a habit has been explained, further details of the habit and some related topics are given as examples of extending the principles involved. Adults could compare the habits and related topics with their own current behaviours and see if any of the habits are worth developing.

Important point
A good way of teaching a child a helpful habit is to role model it yourself!

As mentioned in Part 1, for readers who wish to explain to a child the ideas that are covered in this book, I have written *My Hidden Chimp*, a children's educational book with graphics, exercises and activities.

Chapter 5

Habit 1 – smiling

In this chapter, you will see how the simple act of choosing your expression can affect your mood. Putting on a happy face can have more implications than you think!

- Deciding on how you want to feel
- What effect does smiling have on others?
- Reflections on smiling
- What further significant implications could the principle have?

Deciding on how you want to feel

Let's start with a simple question that I often ask myself. How do you want to feel? This might seem an odd question, but it has implications based in the neuroscience of the mind. If we allow our mind to naturally default to a certain emotion then often, for many of us, this emotion is not a positive one. If we decide that we want to settle on being positive in outlook then the mind will be more prone to use this as its default position. In other words, it is possible to choose our emotional default position and to make a habit of doing this.

What would you say your default position is?

Obviously, if something is concerning us or if we are facing problems of a serious nature, then it's unrealistic to be going around in an inappropriately happy way. However, for most of us, the majority of our days are not traumatising or tough. These are the days when we have a choice as to whether we want to feel good or allow ourselves to default to a more mundane position. If you do decide that you want to feel good, happy or content, or to experience any other specific emotion, then there are ways to improve the chances using neuroscience! To demonstrate this principle of choosing mood according to neuroscience, let's look at facial expression and smiling.

Facial expressions are a very significant way in which we communicate with each other. It is so significant that it is synchronised into the way we feel.

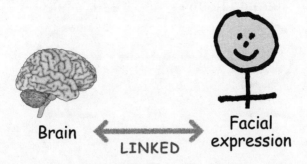

Brain ⟷ LINKED Facial expression

So, if you feel happy, you will automatically show it on your face. Children find it very hard to conceal how they feel, especially when they are lying! As we grow older, we learn to disguise our feelings but often others can see through the disguise. Therefore, the principle is that, if you feel something in your mind, whether a pleasant or an unpleasant emotion, your face will automatically reflect this. Unless you make an effort to conceal your facial expression, others can see how you feel.

So what if we deliberately put an expression on our face, like sadness or happiness – will it make us feel that emotion? In other words, if our faces are so intrinsically synchronised with our minds, can we influence how we feel by forcing a facial expression?

Feeling happy... creates a smile

Making a smile... creates happy feelings

Putting on a smile

The research (and hopefully your own experience, if you try it) gives us the answer. Some researchers have found that, if we maintain a positive facial expression during stressful events, we feel better and also have a slower heart rate when we are recovering.[1]

This putting on of a positive facial expression doesn't have to be only during stressful events. There is evidence that smiling or frowning can make a difference to your mood and produce a positive or negative frame of mind.[2] So, if you force a smile then the chances of feeling happier improve, and if you force a frown then the chances of feeling sad or angry also increase! So, you can influence your mood or how you feel by deciding on what emotion you want to experience and then forming the appropriate facial expression. If we are already in the mood state that we want, then we can enhance it by reinforcing it with a facial expression.

Therefore, if you are enjoying yourself and you deliberately form a smile, it appears to make you enjoy yourself more.[3] The opposite has also been found to be true: if you deliberately form a sad face, you are more likely to feel sadder when you see sad things than if you don't have a sad face.[4] So we can enhance our feelings by deliberately putting on a facial expression.

What effect does smiling have on others?

Smiling at others or receiving smiles from others has also been shown to have positive effects. Some of the research seems obvious, but it is sometimes worth reminding ourselves of it, so that we can act on it. For example, people receive more help when they smile, and smiling at someone can make them more helpful towards you.[5] There is research to show that when parents smile back at a child, the child will continue to smile. So positive attitudes create positive feelings in the child.[6]

This might all seem obvious, but what is going on inside our heads? The response to seeing a smile is based in our Chimp structures, so they are not directly under our control. The amygdala, which is part of the Chimp structures, could be considered as having a powerful battery of energy contained within it, which is in charge of the automatic response that decides on a flight, fight or freeze reaction to situations. It has many other functions, one of which is facial mirroring. When we see another person's face, imaging studies show that our amygdala's response is to imitate the other person's facial expression.[7] [8] This in turn will make us feel that expression.

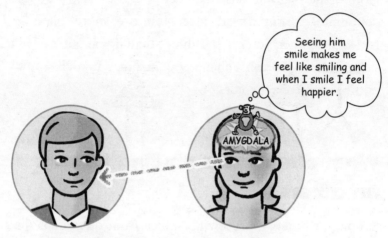

The amygdala mimics a smile

This helps us to understand why our Chimps like positive people with positive facial expressions – because they naturally evoke good feelings in us.[9] They smile, we smile back and our facial expression influences our mind to feel the smile factor. However, it doesn't stop there! Our Chimps continue by jumping to conclusions. For example, when we see a smile on someone else, it doesn't just give us a good feeling; we also rate them as being more intelligent than a non-smiling person.[10]

Important point

The advantage of learning the habit of putting on a smile, or at least a positive expression, can help others and ourselves to feel better and improve relationships.

A lesson for me

When I was working in hospital medicine, we had clinics for those suffering with depression. Many of the doctors I worked with would comment on how they could sometimes feel low themselves when leaving the clinic. I had a very sobering moment in one clinic, when I smiled at a patient as they entered the room. They immediately responded by telling me that seeing me smile made them feel a bit better. Sadly, they went on to tell me that it was the first time they had ever seen me smile. That was a sobering moment for me, and a lesson to learn. I personally think that, for me, a fake smile is worse than no smile! However, with a little bit of thought, there is usually a lot to smile genuinely about, so I do try for a positive expression! If you are not a natural smiler, like me, I recommend a positive expression.

Patient   Doctor

Reflections on smiling

What conclusions, if any, can we draw from this information? What I would recommend is that you try it for yourself. There appears to be a scientific basis for the effect that expression has on mood, so test the theory out and see if it works for you. Getting yourself into a good place by working on positive facial expressions can only have a beneficial effect on those around you. If the theories and research are correct, and the results seem almost self-evident, children will benefit from carers who are smiling, or at least have positive facial expressions.

A game or exercise to teach children about these ideas is to get them to give facial expressions that will evoke feelings in them. So you can ask them to make a happy face, a smiling face, an angry face, a disappointed face and so on. If you ask the child how they feel when they make these faces, they will often say they feel like the face that they are making. When I have tried this with young children (provided they are in a sensible frame of mind!) they have reported back that they experience the emotion of the facial expression.

The main point is to get the child to practise a happy face and to help them to learn to form this as a habit, particularly if they don't naturally feel happy. Children can also appreciate that changing their facial expression can help to make them feel better.

A learnt, positive facial expression, such as greeting people with a smile, can also clearly help children to be perceived by others around them in a more favourable light, which could therefore increase their chances of being more successful in relationships, and life in general.

A happy face needs practice!

What significant further implications could the principle have?

Smiling to alter your mood could be seen as just a novel practice that can work for some, but it has a basis within research on the neuroscience of the brain. Could we extend the principle to alter our default mood or state of mind?

So, putting aside facial expressions for the moment, we could consider the general mood or stance that we take every day as our natural default position. All of us tend to form a habit of being in a certain frame of mind, and this can go unchecked. What is your natural default position?

First, try and recognise exactly what your usual default position is and then you can make changes, if it isn't what you want. If your natural default position is not a helpful one, such as one of restlessness, anxiety, a critical stance or worry, it would be good to alter it to one that would be beneficial, such as enthusiasm, calm, peaceful, grateful or whatever other position that you might want to choose.

This is not as hard as it might at first seem. In essence, it will involve shifting your focus onto things that you know will make you feel the emotions that you want. Of course, it also involves some proactive practical work to remove unhelpful thinking and any unresolved issues.

For children and adults alike, what can be helpful is to have an emotional default position that is beneficial to well-being.

Having a positive outlook as a default position

Having a negative outlook can be just a learnt habit. There are many reasons why this might occur. For example, a negative outlook can occur if a child perceives that they have not quite reached a position where they have obtained unconditional approval or praise from an adult. This can then put them into a frame of mind of, *'No matter how much I try, I can't please an adult.'* Sometimes this can occur when an adult says something like, 'with a bit more effort you could do really well' or, 'this is good, but it could be better'. So, rather than encouraging the child, it can have the opposite effect. It's all about getting the balance!

Some parents praise everything that their children do and what they achieve, but this can have its pitfalls! Very subtly, if a parent praises what a child can do rather than praising the child themselves, then the child can develop the idea that *'I am only as good as what I can achieve'* and may then try to constantly gain approval by proving themselves worthy. Unconditionally letting the child know that they don't have to achieve anything to be loved and respected is the best basis for the child to work from. Being loved and respected *just as we are*, rather than for what we can do or achieve, raises self-esteem and builds self-confidence.

Other examples where a negative outlook can develop include:

- when a child is left with feelings of guilt
- when an adult repeatedly breaks promises to a child or lets them down

- when a child is upset and the experience is dismissed or not addressed

Once a negative outlook is recognised, it can be challenged. Changing to a positive outlook as a natural default position is probably easier than you might imagine. If we can learn what specifically helps us to move our emotions by focusing on what we want to focus on, then we can usually alter our mood state. This will be unique to the individual. Therefore, one way to help a child to be in a good place is to discuss with them how they could make themselves feel better. For example, thinking about things that have made them laugh or future events that they are looking forward to. The child could develop a habit of being happy, grateful or any other stance, provided they have a process to follow that works for them. As with adults, this process will involve addressing any concerns and then shifting their focus onto things that will promote the frame of mind that they want.

Bringing perspective into life can help us to realise that all worries we have are fleeting. They come and they go. Thinking about what today's worries will mean in a year's time can often help us to realise how unimportant they will become. Problems usually resolve or we move on from them with time. Later in the book, habits such as 'talking about your feelings' will help to establish the process of perspective.

Important point
Defaulting to a positive frame of mind can be a learnt habit.

Karl's change of habit

Karl was a man I worked with some time ago. One of his complaints was that he felt unwelcomed by his partner when returning home after work. I asked him to describe what happened. He admitted that when he returned home he would moan and get a lot of frustrations from the day off his chest before settling down. When we considered what effect this had on his partner, he could see why he might be given a less-than-friendly welcome. He put in place a simple behaviour of getting things off his chest before he got home – then, when he arrived home, he gave a big smile and let his partner know how good it was to see them. This changed everything and he reported how easy it was to start the evening feeling welcomed and appreciated. His partner also reported feeling better!

Sometimes very simple habits can make a big difference to you and others around you. How do you come across when meeting others? And more importantly, how do you want to come across?

Summary

- Facial expression and mood state are intricately linked
- Smiling can improve mood state
- Smiling can help improve relationships
- We can work on having an emotionally positive mood state as a default position

Chapter 6

Habit 2 – saying sorry

A simple apology can diffuse many complicated and stressful situations and make everyone feel better.

- Apologies and forgiveness
- Forgiving yourself after a mistake
- How can we help children to apologise effectively?

Apologies and forgiveness

When we receive an apology from someone, areas of our brain give us a sense of forgiveness.[1] It would seem obvious that if someone apologises for something that they did wrong, we would usually feel happier with them and about the situation. However, that isn't always the case and it's worth knowing why, so that we can help our children to understand what saying sorry really means.

First, we can look at some examples from research to get a better picture of the finer details of what apologies involve. Then we can look at ideas about how to make an apology that is meaningful. A lot of research states the expected. For example, if we say sorry and mean it, then people generally forgive us. However, some research results are not quite what we expect to find. Here are some examples of less obvious facts from that research.

Angry situations

If someone has become angry, then only if an apology is perceived as genuine does their blood pressure fall. However, receiving an apology might reduce the person's blood pressure but the feelings of anger usually still remain![2] Why might this be?

When we get an apology, two things happen. The first is that the Human in us accepts the apology in a rational way, which brings the tension down and causes our blood pressure to fall.

The second response is the reaction from the Chimp, which needs time to make sense of the apology and then accept it. Whenever we have become upset about something, our Chimp needs that time to process the emotions we are experiencing. Therefore, the Chimp often continues to feel those emotions for some time after the problem is resolved. It's why many people know that they will feel better once they have had a good night's sleep or have had the chance to get some space.

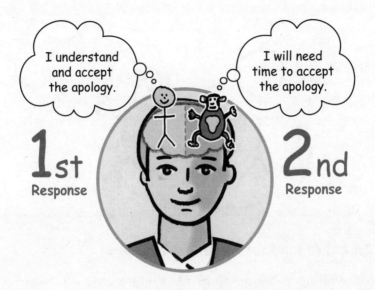

What implication does this have for children who are learning about apologies? It means we have to explain to the child that, once they have apologised to someone, that person might need some time to calm down. It doesn't mean the person hasn't forgiven them – it just means the person's mind needs time to recover. Therefore, it could be useful to keep some distance until the person is ready to engage again. If we can appreciate this, then we can understand ourselves better and also help children not to engage unnecessarily with emotions in others that are settling down.

Key point
Our emotions sometimes need time to follow our logic.

An act of kindness with the apology

More intimate relationships carry more emotion. When a partner apologises for something they have done wrong, they are perceived as sending a message that the relationship means something to them. The person receiving the apology feels valued and also less exploited. Apologising and then doing something to make up for any wrongdoing will help to bring about forgiveness. By adding a kind act to make up for the wrongdoing, the person receiving the kind act usually feels their anger subside and also believes that the wrongdoer won't do the same wrong again.[3]

Regardless of the relationship, there is evidence that, in order to gain forgiveness, offering an apology with *some form of kind act or compensation* is the most effective approach.[4]

This act of compensation seems to be necessary for someone to show humility and then to be accepted and forgiven by the person who has suffered.[5]

What implication could this have for children learning to apologise? It could be helpful to explain that, after saying sorry, it is good to follow this up with actions that back up the sincerity of the apology. As children might find it difficult to think of an act that might compensate, a simpler action might be for them to *ask what they could do to put things right*.

Forgiving yourself after a mistake

Making amends with a kind act can help the person who is apologising forgive themselves, especially if it is a serious error. An example where making amends is very effective occurs in a condition called pathological grief. This has many different presentations and occurs in many different situations. For example, if the driver of a car involved in an accident escaped unharmed but their passenger was injured, the driver could go into a grief stage and get stuck due to feelings of guilt. One way to help to move them forward is for them to do a good deed; somehow the brain sees this as righting the wrong, even though the good deed might not be in any way related to the car accident or the person involved. So doing something good can help to make you feel better if you have upset someone else.

Forgiving yourself can even affect your blood pressure. When we are forgiven, we usually experience a drop in blood pressure, and if we are not forgiven our blood pressure remains high.[6] So it is important to feel that you have been forgiven, not just by the person that you have upset, but also that you have forgiven yourself.

It is also very important to help a child to learn how to forgive themselves. If the child has low self-esteem or holds onto guilt, then they are less likely to be able to learn from a mistake. The child might also find making an apology difficult if they can't forgive themselves and go into defence mode. We will look at how to manage feelings of guilt and forgiving yourself in Chapter 10.

Important point
Performing an act of kindness can help someone to forgive themselves.

Critical point
Unless we learn how to forgive ourselves, we can carry the habit of self-punishment or guilt into adult life

An apology with an explanation

In one experiment, children were asked to judge actors who had done something wrong. Actors who had more elaborate apologies were seen as being less to blame and were given more forgiveness and less punishment. Children also perceived the actors with elaborate explanations as being more remorseful for what they had done[7] and with this understanding came acceptance and forgiveness. This also highlights again that children operate by thinking and not just behaviours.

We can encourage children to offer an explanation with their apology. It might help them to be forgiven more readily if the other person understands why they did what they did.

Jimmy and the annoying little brother
Jimmy was building a house with his play bricks and his younger brother decided to join in. Jimmy resented the interference and asked his brother to go away. The little

brother, feeling rejected, grabbed at the house and demolished it. Jimmy let out a scream and then took a swipe at his little brother, who burst into tears.

Before Jimmy can give an apology, he might need to let his Chimp out first and try to explain why he acted inappropriately. After he has done this, he will be in a better position to offer a sincere apology to his little brother. The same would apply to his little brother! Once Jimmy explains why he was upset, and is listened to and understood, he is much more likely to agree that taking a swipe at his little brother is not acceptable and he could have handled the situation differently.

Important point

Someone is much more likely to give an apology if they have been understood before they reflect on their behaviours and accept that an apology is necessary.

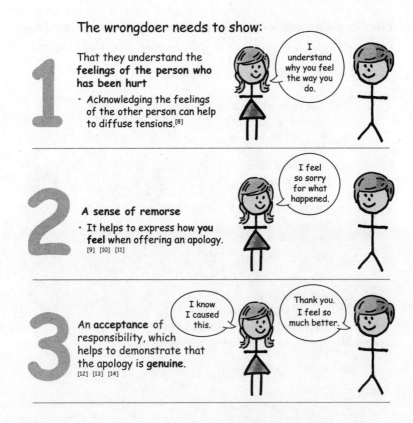

The wrongdoer needs to show:

1

That they understand the **feelings of the person who has been hurt**

- Acknowledging the feelings of the other person can help to diffuse tensions.[8]

I understand why you feel the way you do.

2

A sense of remorse

- It helps to express how **you feel** when offering an apology. [9] [10] [11]

I feel so sorry for what happened.

3

An **acceptance** of responsibility, which helps to demonstrate that the apology is **genuine**. [12] [13] [14]

I know I caused this.

Thank you. I feel so much better.

How can we help children to apologise effectively?

Clearly, sometimes a simple 'sorry' is all that is needed. However, if the situation is more serious, then helping a child learn how to apologise effectively provides them with a great interpersonal skill. When we help the child to have a process for apologising, what we are really doing is developing a Computer programme for them to follow. This way they have a method to help to put things right.

Hopefully you can form a programme that is easy for the child to follow and appropriate for their age and ability!

Here is a suggestion for *the structure of a sincere apology* that anyone could follow, to ensure that they have the best chance of an apology being accepted.

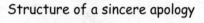

Structure of a sincere apology

1

Start with You
- Say sorry
- Admit any fault
- Take responsibility
- Say how it makes you feel (this shows remorse)
- Explain if possible why it happened (often a Chimp hijack)

I'm sorry, it was my fault.

2

The person
- Ask how they feel
- Acknowledge their feelings
- Ask what can be done to make amends
- Perform an act of kindness towards them

I understand how you feel and I want to make it up to you.

3

Time
- Give the person space to accept the apology
- Forgive yourself – do something good

I will give you some space.

I made a mistake, but I am a good person.

Sometimes we don't know why we do things (usually because of a Chimp hijack!) and therefore it is easier to just say 'I don't know why I did it', rather than to rationalise and learn to lie.

Important point

Please remember the Chimp model is not an excuse. You can't just shrug your shoulders and say, 'It was my Chimp'. You are fully responsible for your Chimp.

Children and taking responsibility

Helping a child to accept responsibility and accountability for their actions is constructive, but only if the child can do something positive with this accountability. A problem can arise if the child believes they are never going to be forgiven. This leaves them in an impossible position, and lingering guilt or lowered self-esteem are likely outcomes. Helping the child to see how to get over a mistake and how to learn from it will help them learn how to accept responsibility and accountability for their own actions. If we don't help a child to see how they can get over a mistake or misdemeanour, it is much more likely that the child will try to avoid taking responsibility.

Important point

For a child to learn to accept responsibility and accountability for their own actions, they need to have a positive and constructive action plan for getting over mistakes.

Telling lies

We looked at magical thinking and magical undoing in Chapter 4 and can now expand on this. The way that very young children think is, 'If I believe something, then it must have happened and it is true, and if I don't believe something, then it can't have happened and it is not true'. This is a way to protect the child from accepting responsibility and also avoiding punishment or consequences. It can also be used to deal with events that have not gone the way the child wanted them to, so that they remember them differently from reality. It is a very childish way of thinking and is usually shown by very young children who cannot yet see something from another person's perspective. They simply believe that everyone believes the same as they do. The Chimp circuits are at work!

These Chimp circuits cannot work with reality and try to reject anything that doesn't fit with what they want to see or hear. As we get older, the Human circuits bring reality and responsibility into play. Magical thinking then becomes recognised as inappropriate by most children, who are able to replace magical thinking with deceit and lies to manage difficult situations. Lying can then become a habit. Magical thinking usually converts to lying between three and five years of age.

As the child continues to mature, then they learn the new behaviour of accepting responsibility and consequences, but this needs encouragement. Breaking the habit of lying means implementing a new habit of accepting responsibility and dealing with consequences. This can be achieved by talking through the process with a child, and getting them to think ahead to see that the consequences of telling the truth are far better than the consequences of lying.

Summary

- Forgiving yourself is very important
- Apologies that have acts of kindness attached are more likely to be accepted

- A person's Chimp might need some time to accept an apology
- Acknowledging the person's feelings shows understanding
- A critical factor to receiving forgiveness is showing remorse
- Having a structured plan for saying sorry can cover all the helpful points

Chapter 7

Understanding and managing mishaps

Mishaps are part of everyday life. They have many causes, such as accidents, bad luck, lapses in attention and even acts of nature. They result in unwelcome outcomes or challenges, which can cause unnecessary stress. Understanding and managing mishaps can lead to constructive outcomes and remove stress.

- What could be the cause of a mishap?
- The big question: what do you want as the outcome of a mishap?
- What response do you want to see from your child?
- Have you got your response ready?

What could be the cause of a mishap?

In order to appreciate the next point, I want to begin with four scenarios based on the same situation. The scenarios will all have the same outcome, but the causes behind the outcome will be very different.

The point is therefore about reflecting on how the adult

could ***respond to the cause*** rather than ***respond to the outcome.***

The broken vase

A child has broken a very precious vase. Although the Chimp in the adult might be distressed at the broken vase and want to react to the situation, the Human in the adult is likely to want to ask, 'Why did it happen?' before responding.

Here are the four different scenarios for the cause of the broken vase. I am deliberately using extreme scenarios, in order to clarify the principle involved.

Scenario 1

The child unintentionally knocked over the vase due to an accident.

- A friend's dog that was greeting the child jumped up and accidentally pushed the child into the vase.
- The child then became distressed.

Scenario 2

The child unintentionally knocked over the vase because of poor coordination.

- The child suffers from a movement disorder and when walking past the vase could not control their balance.
- The child then became distressed.

Scenario 3

The child unintentionally knocked over the vase because they failed to concentrate on where they were going.

- The child was very excited and getting ready for a trip to the seaside, so failed to watch where they were going.
- The child then became distressed.

Scenario 4

The child intentionally broke the vase.

- The child ran towards the vase, picked it up and threw it against the wall.
- The child now stands defiant.

What do these four scenarios represent?

Scenario 1 represents an accident

We all have accidents, and although we apologise for them, they are usually not anybody's fault. They happen outside of our control.

Scenario 2 represents poor coordination that ALL children suffer from

All children are in various stages of physical development. They have to learn coordination. They might not suffer with any specific disorder, but their coordination is not fully developed and they will inevitably be clumsy at times. They cannot help this. This scenario is there to remind us, as adults, that children have physical limitations. Research has shown that children with poor coordination development can suffer from depressive and anxiety symptoms and are also less likely to join in play activities.[1]

Scenario 3 represents the psychological limitations of a healthy child

The ability to retain and change focus is one of the functions of the dorsolateral prefrontal cortex (Human).[2] The ability to retain focus on an instruction, such as 'Please watch the vase', is only possible with a mature brain. It is not surprising, therefore, that children struggle to concentrate and retain focus. A child's developing mind does not have the ability to see consequences easily, if at all. Therefore, playing a boisterous game near a precious vase *would not seem unwise* to a child. It might be worth remembering these points when assessing how a child is doing. I am not in any way suggesting that we allow children to run riot and have no responsibility. What I am suggesting is that an adult bears in mind the limitations that a child will naturally struggle with, before responding to an incident.

Scenario 4 represents a child who intentionally meant to break the vase

We would have to be mind-readers to know exactly why the child did this, and therefore need to ask questions.

There are two possibilities: the child was emotionally hijacked by their Chimp and didn't agree with their actions, or they purposefully wanted to break the vase.

Why would someone deliberately break the vase?

On purpose	Emotional hijack
Purposefully wanted to break the vase	Emotionally hijacked by their Chimp and didn't agree with the action.

We all get hijacked by our Chimps but must accept responsibility for this. For a child, this is particularly difficult because by accepting responsibility we are saying that we will try to avoid this situation happening again. This means Chimp management. As adults, it means working with the Human parts of our mind and having a fully functioning Computer to support us, but the child does not have this option. A reminder again! Their Human is not fully formed and their Computer can't be fully functional because it has little experience to learn from and therefore to build wisdom from. We need to act as their Human and also help them to programme their Computer.

A child who wilfully broke the vase would need some real understanding to get to the cause of their actions.

Let's look at what we can do to avoid this happening again.

Your role

At this point, it is worth considering how you could help. What could you have done to prevent the child from being put in the situation in the first place? For example, could you have made it safer and impossible for the child to get anywhere near the vase?

The vase just represents something important. I will leave you to think of the more abstract potential pitfalls it could represent, such as playing in a safe setting, supervised when with animals, limited access to sweets and so on.

It's always worth asking what part you might have played in a mishap, so that you too can learn from the event. As with the child, there is no point in feeling guilty or reprimanding yourself. It's much better to accept that the situation has happened and ask what the way forward is.

The big question: what do you want as the outcome of a mishap

Whenever a mishap occurs, it's worth asking yourself *what you want* as the outcome of this mishap, for both your child and yourself.

The Child

Do you want to punish the child?

Do you want to get the child to learn from this?

Do you want to explore with the child what could have been avoided?

Yourself

How do you want to be?

You could ask yourself a rhetorical question: Do you want to be calm and reasonable, or reactive and impulsive?

The outcome

What do you want as a result of your interaction and response to the situation?

The answers to these questions are in your hands and would be useful to reflect on. When you know what you want as the outcome, you will have a guide to your response.

It can be helpful to first ask yourself what the child intended to do.

If you can appreciate that the child has been put in a tough position by the very physical nature of the machine that they are working within, then ideas of punishment or reprimand might not only seem inappropriate but could be potentially damaging. It could be seen as akin to asking someone to fly and then getting upset if they can't manage it. I am not suggesting that children should not be given some element of responsibility. However, the child will need guidance on how they should respond. The child themselves might have inappropriate responses when an unintentional event occurs. For example, they might feel guilty or condemn themselves, instead of being apologetic and then using the experience as a learning point.

The example of the broken vase is offered to help you to reflect on the intentions of the child. It's worth considering what caused the mishap to occur, so that your own response is appropriate.

Summary of causes

- Unintentional
  - Accidental
  - Physical limitations
  - Psychological limitations

- Intentional
  - Emotional hijack
  - Purposeful

Bear in mind that children are often:

- Not fully physically coordinated
- Lacking in awareness

- Working from an impulsive Chimp basis
- Lacking in emotional management
- Lacking in experience and wisdom

It is expected that every child will make many errors that need apologies, but all mishaps have potential learning points.

What response do you want to see from your child?

What can you, as a parent, do to help the child to learn?

Do you want to see fear, remorse, distress, indifference or some other emotion? If the child is left to form their own response then it might not be a constructive or appropriate one. One way to help a child to programme their Computer is to play a game to enact the response that you would like.

Make up some scenarios that you know the child is likely to encounter, especially ones that you might find stressful yourself. You can then either role-play the scenarios, or help the child to enact the scenarios using their toys to represent you and them.

For example:

- Being naughty in a public place
- Being difficult when asked to go to bed
- Acting silly and not listening
- Carrying a cup of water that is full and impossible not to spill

Get them to go through the steps of what you will say and how they will respond. Then discuss any learning points and other situations where the same scenario or similar might occur.

Using videos of a cartoon or similar, in which accidents or incidents occur, can help. It might help to discuss with the child why things happened and who should apologise and how this could be done.

Have you got your response ready?

At this point we could ask if you have got a response that you have programmed into your own Computer for when your child misbehaves or needs to apologise. Being responsible for raising a child is rarely easy and can create stress.

Important point
Adults frequently become stressed because they have not got a programmed response ready for when a child misbehaves.

> ### *A suggested exercise for you to try*
>
> *This exercise could be performed with a friend for feedback. When a child makes a mistake, work out what response will help and what response won't help. Map out your own Computer programme and then try it out, so that you have rehearsed a response to the mishap or misbehaviour.*
>
> *What about the case where the child has deliberately chosen to perform a misdemeanour? What will be your desired response? If you do not have a Computer programme then your Chimp will take the lead and react to the situation.*
>
> *The most important foundation for your stability is to be in a good place yourself at the start of each day!*

The apples and the box

Many years ago, I had a small group of apple trees in my garden that had produced a large number of apples that autumn. I was with two friends and we decided to finish picking the apples that were still hanging on the trees. So we took a cardboard box and began collecting the apples in it. When it was full and almost impossible to pick up we decided to take it back to the house. Halfway there, the bottom of the box fell out and the apples rolled everywhere. One friend and myself fell about laughing at our own stupidity. It was obvious the box wasn't going to carry the weight. The other friend was so angry at the time we had wasted.

It made me realise that sometimes it's easier to laugh at mistakes and your own stupidity than to react seriously to them. Helping a child laugh at stupid mistakes puts things into perspective. Helping the child to see that, *it* was a stupid mistake but *they* are not stupid, will make mistakes easier to manage. Laughing *with* the child is even better, and if it is about your own mistakes, even better still!

Summary

- Looking at the cause of a mishap helps us to understand why it happened
- Having a response ready for both the child and adult is very beneficial to both
- Being in a good place yourself is the basis for managing a mishap by a child

Chapter 8

Habit 3 – being kind to others

Being kind to others – so long as there are no strings attached – builds good feelings in both the recipient and the giver. In turn, it's good to practise being kind to yourself.

- Kind acts
- What happens when we are kind to someone?
- Different ways of being kind
- Being kind to yourself
- Meanness turned around

Kind acts

Being kind towards others can be an unselfish act or an act for personal gain. The two generally go hand in hand, because when we are kind to others it usually gives us a good feeling.

However, altruistic acts are different to acts that have conditions attached. It helps children to know the difference, because some adults still haven't separated the two. Some adults offer gifts with 'strings attached' in order to influence others using emotional means. Effectively, these are not gifts but a means of control. For example, a gift of money would have strings attached if you then check to see how they spend it. That is not really a kind act! Giving a gift and then taking it back or having a say on what they do with it is controlling. Offering to help someone and then letting them know that they owe you a favour is not a kind act, it's more like a business negotiation!

The habit of having strings attached to an act of kindness usually results in conflict and resentment and can be the source of strained relationships. We can help children not to carry this habit into adult life if we take time to explain the difference between being kind, and being kind with strings attached.

The idea that when we do something pleasant for someone, they should do the same back is about emotional fairness. A sense of emotional fairness and justice is not actually found in the Human circuits but is found in the Chimp circuits of the brain, and is seen in many species, including monkeys.[1]

This sense of fairness and balance means that if our Chimp kicks in when we are doing a kind act, it might add the strings and demand that there should be some trade-off.

The Human circuits work more by way of morals and compassion and therefore tend not to add any strings to a kind act. The idea that what you do is what you expect others to do might seem reasonable, but it is flawed logic. It is seen in the old adage that, if I meet a lion and don't intend to harm it, then it won't harm me! So, you could argue, what's the point of being kind? Apart from the altruistic aspect, there are still benefits to you.

What happens when we are kind to someone?

The evidence is clear that not only does the person to whom we are being kind feel good, but *we* also get a sense of well-being.[2] The main hormone that helps us to be generous is oxytocin and experiments show that if we boost this hormone in people then they become more generous.[3]

So oxytocin helps us to develop a sense of well-being. Even if we do not expect any return for our kindness, the evidence is that, when we are kind to someone, they will see us in a good light and also will be much more likely to do kind acts for us.[4] [5]

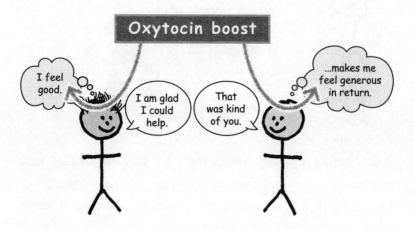

Different ways of being kind

There are various ways of being kind to someone and each can be learnt as a habit. Examples of being kind include:

- Offering kind or encouraging words
- Considerate and supportive behaviour
- Listening to someone
- Being thoughtful
- Putting someone else first
- Showing appreciation and acknowledging what someone has done for you
- Giving a gift without strings attached!
- Pleasantly surprising someone

With some reflection I am sure you can think of many ways of being kind to those around you. Apart from improving your own well-being, it is very likely to improve relationships.

Developing a habit of being kind is about programming your Computer to default into a kindness mode whenever you meet people. Sometimes it is not what we say that is the problem – the problem is what we do not say. Very often, people tell me that they forgot to tell someone what they mean to them or how much they appreciate them. But it isn't difficult to develop a habit of being kind.

Suggested helpful habit

Try to greet someone with a genuinely pleasant comment.

Being kind to yourself

You can also be kind to yourself. One way to help with self-esteem is to praise yourself for the things that you have done and the values you possess. Too often, I see people constantly criticising themselves with no mention of praise. If you tend to do this, it's worth asking if it is really helpful.

Children can also learn to be very self-critical, and this unhelpful habit can persist. Teaching them how to be kind to themselves is a productive basis for adult life. For a child, approval from an adult is a critical aspect to gain validity. Therefore, it helps not just to praise a child when you see them performing an act of kindness, but also to approve of them learning to praise themselves.

Important point

Praising yourself can be based on doing your best, not just achieving.

> I am proud of myself for living out my values.

Meanness turned around

Seeing their child being mean to other children concerns some parents and carers. Whatever form this meanness takes, the important point is to recognise that it is natural, even though it is unwelcome. The Chimp will try and protect territories, such as toys, possibly dominate by trying to be better than others and will often use violence to achieve this dominance.

One way of making sure that someone will keep their distance from you in the future, so that you can protect your territory, is to make their encounter with you unpleasant! If you can see that this is what the Chimp within your child is doing, then it makes sense for them to be as unpleasant as possible towards other children. This can include biting, attacking and any other natural-but-unacceptable activity.

To move things forward, first *accept* that this is normal behaviour for a Chimp, even though it is unacceptable for society. I think it is important not to see the behaviour for more than what it is. The child is learning what it can and can't do. The way a young child can do this is by carrying out behaviours and seeing which ones work to its advantage. We can therefore work with all three different systems to help the child: the Chimp, the Human and the Computer.

The Chimp will work purely with behaviours and looks for rewards or unrewarding outcomes.

Behaviour input

So disapproving of actions the child takes can be effective if, for example, following an unhelpful act of meanness by the child you withhold affection, withhold toys or place restrictions on activities. Another way is to tell them that you are upset and that they need to apologise to you and ask them to give you some space. I personally think it's important to remind them that you still love them, despite their actions.

The problem with working purely with behaviours is that we are not helping the child to develop the Human parts of the mind, which are present but not developed. Therefore, in order to bring the Human circuits into action, we can discuss with the child why we are finding things unacceptable and why there are consequences to actions. Explaining in a calm and measured manner will help the child to move towards the Human circuits.

Important point

Be careful: if your explanation is given by using a lot of emotion, it is likely to keep the child in Chimp mode.

If the child understands the Chimp model, then it is possible to explain that they have a choice about whether to be Human or a Chimp. You could ask them directly if they want to be Human or Chimp and what kind of behaviours they would like to have. Let's hope they say Human! Remind the child of how strong the Chimp is and how it can hijack them and try to fool them into believing they are a Chimp and not Human. My youngest student of the Chimp model was two, and she got it perfectly and was able to use the model going forward.

To bring the Computer system into play would entail sitting the child down, when they are not in an emotional state and you are not addressing any misdemeanour, and then helping to programme the Computer with a suitable response.

Let's look at how you could manage your Chimp so that there is no meanness.

You could approach this by asking them how they **would want to react** if someone annoys or upsets them, and how they wouldn't want to react. For example, they might want to let a brother, sister or friend know how they feel but not be mean or unkind to them. If you explain that their Chimp is very likely to react and therefore we need a learnt response to manage the Chimp, it could help the child to distance themselves from the Chimp. You could ask them: how could you manage your Chimp so that you are not mean?

A programmed response

This programmed response has to be feasible and practical. Every child is unique, so this means finding what will work for your child and yourself. For example, if a child is overwhelmed by emotion, asking them to find an adult and tell them how they feel, rather than reacting, will only work for some children. Those children it will work for would still need to practise this behaviour in order to ensure it is well ingrained as a first response. Alternative possible programmed behaviours, depending on the age of the child, could include:

- Preparing before an event – for example, deciding on which toys they will share and removing those that they don't want to share before a friend arrives
- Learning a fixed response for removing frustration, such as being allowed to shout into the air
- Being assertive and explaining to the other child what they do and don't want to happen and how they feel

Apart from having a learnt response, we can also help the child to form beliefs to place into the Computer.

Examples of beliefs that could prevent meanness

One difficulty when working with children is that we have to respect that their minds are not fully developed and allow for this. So younger children will work much more by using behaviours, and older children will move towards cognitive (thinking) ways of working. Can we help children with this transition? Yes! This leads us onto the topic of 'theory of mind', which is covered in the next chapter. Understanding it will help us to generally appreciate the development of the mind of a child.

Summary

- A kind act has no strings attached
- Being kind is a source of well-being
- There are lots of ways of being kind
- Be kind to yourself

Chapter 9

Theory of mind

In order to understand how someone else feels, we need to have what is called a 'theory of mind'. This is an important aspect of child development.

- Theory of mind
- A recognised order for learning theory of mind
- The early foundations
- Some later foundations
- What other ways are there to help children develop a theory of mind?

Theory of mind

Theory of mind simply means that we can understand what is happening in another person's mind. For example, we can appreciate what they are feeling, what they perceive is happening, what their intentions are and predict their responses to situations. It gives us the ability to see another person's point of view and therefore to read people. Theory of mind is one of the main emotional skills that predicts future success in all areas of our lives.[1] This increase in success stands to reason, because if you can understand another person then you are more likely to be able to communicate with them, learn from them, and form meaningful relationships with them, along with a multitude of other things.

Theory of mind

I think I understand what is happening in your mind.

If theory of mind is so important, it begs the question, can we help to develop this in a child? If we could do this, then it might help to give them a head start in life. Happily, the answer is that we can!

We will start by looking at how a child develops theory of mind and then look at ways of helping to awaken and develop it.

A recognised order for learning theory of mind

Children usually learn theory of mind in a recognised order. Experts differ in how they classify the way we develop theory of mind. For simplicity, here are some examples showing a general order in the way that children learn it.

- Understanding their own desires and emotions
- Gaining insight into the fact that people do not always feel the same as they do

- Accepting that people act differently because they want different things
- Understanding that people can think differently when interpreting the same situation, and act differently according to what they think is happening
- Recognising that what they can see in their mind, others can't see. Realising that they have to explain, with details, what they are seeing or recalling for others to fully understand
- Appreciating what beliefs and false beliefs are
- Recognising that people can believe things that are not true and can act on false beliefs
- Gaining insight into deception and empathy
- Accepting that people don't always tell them their true feelings and that they can be deceived

Most children will have some level of ability and skills in all aspects of theory of mind by the age of six, but the variance is great. All of us can continue to develop these skills throughout life.

As you read the points that are being discussed, you might want to think about ways in which you can help your child to develop or strengthen the skill being learnt. If you are stuck for ideas, I have offered some suggestions towards the end of the chapter and some suggestions are interspersed as we go along.

A caution

I would like to stress the need to work from where the child has reached, in terms of their mind development.

I mentioned that the mind develops through stages, and we therefore have to work with the mind that the child has and not expect it to do something it can't do. A child can only reach certain stages by a certain age. Of course, there will be variation in development, but to try and encourage a child to do something they can't possibly do is obviously unhelpful.

A well-known experiment might help to clarify this.[2]

Some three-year-old children were given a tube of Smarties. Before one opened the tube, the adult asked the child what they expected to find inside the tube and the child answered 'Smarties'. However, when the child opened the tube, they found pencils inside.

The child was then asked two questions. The first question was: 'If another child sees the tube, what do you think that this child will think is inside the tube?' The three-year-old child usually answered, 'They will say pencils'. The second question is: 'When *you* first saw the tube, what did *you* think was inside it?' The three-year-old child usually answered, 'pencils'.

The experiment was then repeated with four-year-olds. When asked the first question, the four-year-olds answered differently. They usually said the child would expect to see 'Smarties'. The four-year-old child's answer to the second question was usually, 'I was expecting to see Smarties'.

This difference in answers and insight occurred naturally over the space of one year. The three-year-olds could not adjust their thinking back to before they discovered the reality of what was in the tube, and they also couldn't appreciate that other three-year-olds would be fooled. They effectively believed that whatever knowledge they had, others would have too.

It can be seen from this example that it would be wise to be careful when helping children to enhance their theory of mind that we don't confuse or upset them by trying to get them to do something their mind is unable to comprehend. It is worth explaining things to them, but I am just offering a caution to consider that, even with explanation, the child might struggle to follow your reasoning.

The early foundations

Specialists in this field all agree that theory of mind begins during early childhood, but disagree as to exactly what age it occurs.[3] Rather than debate this, we can look at the fundamentals and those readers who are interested can follow up with the references.

Infants typically start by copying the actions of others.

Children begin by copying...
...and they don't tend to stop!

They then begin to appreciate that other people have feelings and recognise that these feelings are connected to facial expressions. The infant progresses by learning to use words to describe these feelings.

If we pause here to reflect on this, then we can see some significant possibilities to help develop these naturally occurring stages.

Learning about how people feel through facial expressions

Often, adults can tell how another person feels through their facial expressions. Helping a young child identify and name them is a good first step towards developing a theory of mind.

Action point

*For example, we could encourage children to **copy** what we do. As they copy what we do, we could encourage them to **say what they think** our facial expression is telling them about how we feel.*

Sad   Happy

*Most importantly, we can help them to **verbalise** what this means. Getting the child to mimic different expressions or to read your expression is always fun! Helping children to use words to describe emotions will not only give an explanation to them but will also increase their language skills. With older children we can also consider body language. Different simple body language positions can be taught by asking the child to try and demonstrate how they would act for different emotions that they are experiencing.*

Different feelings

As the foundations of theory of mind develop, infants become aware that people can have different feelings to the ones that the infants themselves are experiencing. People have different likes and dislikes, and therefore people act differently.

Action point

Discussion with the child about people being different in what they like and dislike will help the child to appreciate that we are all diverse. This can easily be expanded to understanding how people feel differently when doing the same thing. For example, if the child were asked to tell you how they feel when they are doing something they really like, you could then explain that another child might not like doing this activity, so how would they feel? Getting the child to discuss these notions is very beneficial in helping them to grasp these concepts.

Different motives

At some point, the child will come to recognise that actions are linked to motives and that people act according to what they want.

> ## Action point
> *Learning to guess at 'what people might do' in different circumstances could be made into a game. For example, guessing at what someone might do if they want a bag of sweets but haven't got the money to pay for them. Or guessing what someone might do if they have accidently damaged a toy. Discussing how everyone might react differently and even how some people might act dishonestly, will help in understanding people. Children develop the concept of deception at about five years old. Discussing deception can lead to ideas about ethics and morals.*

Actions and their emotional consequences

Alongside recognising that actions are linked to motives, the child will begin to appreciate that there are consequences not only to actions but also to emotions that are being experienced.

> **Action point**
>
> *Discussing with the child the actions they might take and the effects these actions will have on others will help them to appreciate consequences.*

By the time children have reached the age of five, many aspects of theory of mind will be present.[4] Many experts agree that it is at this age that they start to contemplate what other people are feeling and thinking.

Some later foundations

Once the child begins to appreciate differences that individuals experience in thinking, motives and emotions, they then develop more complex theory of mind skills. For example, the child learns that their own experience needs to be explained in detail if someone else is to understand what they have seen or heard.

> **Action point**
>
> *A game can easily be made out of this by letting them watch a scenario on a video clip and then helping them to select the relevant points that would help someone else understand what they saw.*

A higher skill is to appreciate that someone can believe something that isn't true and then act on this misbelief. Many people still become confused by another adult's behaviour because they have not appreciated that it is based on misinformation or untruths.

An even higher skill is to accept that, even confronted with the facts, some people will still not believe them. The idea that someone can't accept the truth is very hard for most of us to manage!

As the child advances in skill levels they also come to realise that people can deceive them about their true feelings and motives, which can then lead the child to interact inappropriately.

What other ways are there to help children develop a theory of mind?

Whatever we do, children will naturally develop theory of mind. The brain will lay down pathways during this emotional skill development and some experiences are likely to help the child to develop these pathways.[5]

Here are some further ideas and suggestions for aiding the development of a child, starting with the basic levels of learning and then moving into more difficult learning concepts for older children. If any of these suggestions seem relevant to you, then enjoy them! If not, try to invent other ways you feel could help a child.

Expression and words

Helping a very young child to be able to understand and express their own emotions with *appropriate* words is a starting point. The use of different words such as 'annoyed', 'frustrated' or 'disappointed' to explain more clearly how they feel will help them to understand themselves better. Try to offer scenarios that clearly would lead most people to a predictable emotion.

Some easy examples:

- A party that they were looking forward to being cancelled – disappointed
- Spilling a drink over a favourite book – upset
- Not being able to do something that they usually can do, like tie a shoelace – frustrated
- Finishing a hard job like tidying up – satisfied
- Receiving an unexpected present – surprised and pleased
- Doing a very good job – proud
- Being puzzled and wanting to know more – intrigued

Expanding on the child's vocabulary can help them to better communicate with others. For example, if they can learn to distinguish the differences between love and like, angry and frustrated, and concerned and anxious, they can then communicate more effectively.

Role-modelling

Children naturally mimic adults or other children. By encouraging and directing this in a role-play, the child can establish constructive habits.

For example, very young children will happily mimic you as you tidy up, if you give them encouragement. This can help to form a helpful habit of being tidy. It could be fun for the child if you first agree to make a mess, with the intent of tidying up.

Older children could be asked about role-playing someone they respect or admire, and discussing what it is they admire about them and how this could be demonstrated in the role-play.

In both cases, role-modelling can be extended to discuss what the role model is thinking and why they are thinking this, enhancing theory of mind. This will help to enforce the formation of the constructive habit.

Talking about someone else's feelings

For an older child, we can extend the idea of understanding someone else's behaviour. For example, you could ask the child to imagine being a bus driver and ask them to be careful to watch for anyone who might suddenly walk out into the road. It's a short step to discuss that we need to be careful because other people might not always be thinking. You could also ask them to tell you how the bus driver is feeling if the roads are very busy or he is stuck in a traffic jam and is running late.

Children could be encouraged to make up or write scenarios based on feelings, and also to offer solutions on how to turn negative or unhelpful feelings into positive ones. Discussion about how to respond to other people when they are experiencing or demonstrating different emotions can also be helpful.

One way to help a child to think about other people's feelings is to ask them to draw a picture of a scenario and then fill in thought bubbles.

What are they feeling and thinking?

Explanations help with understanding

A big step forward is when the child appreciates that, if we explain things and offer reasons for our actions, the actions are more likely to be accepted. For example, if they took a toy from a younger sibling just before the sibling went downstairs, the sibling is likely to protest. However, if the child explained to the sibling that they are helping the sibling because it could be dangerous for them to carry the toy downstairs and they will give the toy back at the bottom of the stairs, the action is more likely to be accepted.

A multitude of possibilities

There are numerous possible topics for helping to develop theory of mind in children of all ages. They are fundamentally based on thinking, discussion and reflection. Here are more topics that you could consider:

- People act differently depending on what they think is happening
- Actions and emotions that are expressed have consequences for the person and others around them
- Someone might act on a false belief
- Sometimes people will not accept the facts
- People can mislead or deceive you
- Understanding why people are sometimes surprised

Summary

- Theory of mind is the ability to understand what is happening in someone else's mind

- Having the ability to operate with a theory of mind improves all aspects of our lives
- There are many ways in which we can help children to develop theory of mind

Chapter 10

Habit 4 – talking about your feelings

Talking about your feelings and also situations can help you to manage them and give perspective. This expression of emotions is well known to be very therapeutic and also helps to stabilise the mind. This chapter looks at how to form a habit of talking through your feelings; a habit that can be learnt at any age.

- What happens when we talk about our feelings?
- What proof is there that talking helps?
- Troubleshooting
- Making time to talk

What happens when we talk about our feelings?

One habit that helps to stabilise the mind is to talk through your feelings. By expressing your feelings, the mind has the chance to do a number of things. The first is to give an opening for your Chimp to air issues that are bothering it or causing it distress. When the Chimp is allowed to vent its feelings, the Human part of the brain has a chance to listen and process what is happening. Many people know that, when they talk about their problems or ideas, they listen to themselves talking and often see things differently. What they are doing is giving their Human a chance to use logic and perspective. So when feelings are expressed, the Chimp speaks and the Human listens.

Important point
When we talk out loud, our Human listens and brings a different perspective

Children are no different to adults in needing to express their feelings. However, their Human is not very well developed and so usually they still cannot bring perspective or logic to the situation. *Being the Human to a child's Chimp is an important role for an adult who is with them*. When you watch adults who are effective in helping children that are in distress, they frequently follow a sequence:

- They *listen* first and get a clear picture of what the child *perceives* is happening
- They show *compassionately* that they have *understood* the child
- They help the child to *talk* about their *fears and remove these*
- *They find what* **conclusions** the child might have reached and then *alter these conclusions* if they are not correct
- Finally, the adult offers *ways to move forward*

When I started working in child psychiatry, one of the first things to strike me was the depth of thinking that very young children are capable of. It immediately made me realise just how important it was to listen and understand what was happening in their minds. No matter what fear or conclusion the child had, I learnt to take it seriously. Children clearly welcome explanations that they can follow. Moving from working with adults to working with children had many obvious differences, but I came to appreciate that children of all ages welcome discussion, no differently to adults.

What proof is there that talking helps?

There are a number of areas that have been researched. I have selected a few of these as examples of how talking about your feelings can help you to manage them.

Talking out loud, either alone or with someone else, reduces stress levels. On the other hand, bottling things up can lead to intrusive thoughts that just won't go away. By talking things through, it has been found that if the same stressor is met again, the person will deal with it better than the person who did not talk things through.[1] This research is based on the completion hypothesis,[2] which states that by talking we come to make sense of stressful events. During talking we create words that explain our feelings. We can then make sense of what we feel and use this to help others to understand us.

Another advantage of talking things out loud is that we rationalise events and feel less threatened. This can change the emotions that we feel towards the event.

Sometimes when we talk about something that is stressing us, it can initially make us feel worse. However, if we keep talking about the situation then we usually pick up in mood and unwelcome thoughts disappear. [3]

Troubleshooting

What if a child finds it very hard to express their fears and thoughts?

Some children will find it difficult to speak about their thoughts or feelings. There can be a number of reasons for this. Here are a few suggestions for helping them to express their concerns or to talk about a distressing event. I hope you'll find one or more that resonate.

Normalising

Everybody finds it comforting to know that what they are experiencing or how they are reacting is normal. Our Chimp brains are built to *react* to situations. While that isn't always helpful, it is normal. Letting the child know that having difficulty expressing how they feel is normal and then showing them possible ways of getting through this can be comforting. Always let them know you are there with them. When possible, it is very helpful to let them know that other children have experienced what they are going through and things worked out in the end.

Paintings and toys

Another helpful method for a child to explain what happened or how they feel is to let them draw or paint a picture and to tell a story from the picture. The picture depicts the scene or experience that the child has experienced and they might then be able to attribute feelings to the people in the picture. Asking the child to put significant people or events in the picture will often make explaining easier. Some people use toys to enact an event.

Doing an activity while talking

Sometimes a difficult conversation can be made easier if the centre of attention is on something else and the conversation becomes secondary. By focusing on some task or activity, such as preparing a meal, going for a walk, playing with the dog or even painting or colouring a picture together, the child is likely to feel less pressured.

The best friend

Another way to allow the child to express difficult feelings is to ask what their best friend would say. The child can then tell you what their best friend would say about how they feel and about what has happened.

If the child finds this exercise difficult, an alternative is to ask them to tell a story about a boy or girl who has gone through the same experience as them. They can then answer questions on how this boy or girl felt.

Changing the situation

Sometimes asking the child what they would like to change or how they would make things different can help to get them to talk and express how they feel. Occasionally children will even tell you what they think would help and how things could get better – it's just a question of asking them.

The triple-question option

When asking questions that might be awkward to answer, giving options and then narrowing down can be an easier way to reach difficult-to-talk-about topics. For example, let's assume the child is worried about something at school and you suspect this but are not getting any answers. You can begin by asking them to let you know if the problem is one of the following, but not to tell you which one. Your offers could be:

- Bullying
- In trouble with the teacher
- Feeling they can't do something

If the answer is 'yes' then all you have to do is eliminate the alternatives one by one. If you haven't got a 'yes,' then invent three other scenarios. I have used this approach with young people and it usually works each time, as they relax.

Making time to talk

There is nothing better for bringing a person closer to a child than being able to have protected talking time. For them and you this will be special. Forming a habit of talking things through will help the child to become aware of how helpful this is for getting things into perspective. If the child finds it difficult to engage then you could try asking them to keep a diary or a drawing book and to discuss what they have written or drawn for that day.

Please remember to try and ensure that you are in the right frame of mind when engaging. It is important that the time is seen as sacrosanct. Occasionally it is worth sharing your own experiences from childhood, which might help the child to realise that you might have felt the same way when you were a child.

More than one conversation

Difficult topics or events can take several conversations and it's worth limiting time so that the child can assimilate what is being discussed. Frequently the child might need to go over a topic again before they can move on. This is a time for the parent to be patient and accept that the first few discussions might not bring about any change or resolution. If the child finds it difficult to talk, then engagement can be made by first asking about more everyday things such as, 'How was school today?' or 'What would you like to do this weekend?'

Managing feelings of guilt

Beating yourself up and hanging onto guilt are both very destructive habits. They often appear as the source of very low self-esteem and depressive feelings. Therefore, it is important to know how to manage any feelings of guilt. Children can suffer severely with feelings of guilt, and both children and adults can learn how to manage such feelings.

Guilt is an emotion that is experienced when we believe

we have done something wrong, been negligent or could have prevented something. Guilt, therefore, is acting as a prompt to tell us that we should be doing something and not just sitting there. Guilt isn't meant to be endured or something to become preoccupied with, but rather acted upon. There are several constructive ways to remove guilt.

Removing guilt begins by appreciating and ***accepting*** that we all make mistakes or do something wrong from time to time. This is not an excuse, but rather an understanding that we do get Chimp hijacks or just lose focus. Once we have accepted this, we can move forward. We can ***apologise*** and perform a kind or compensatory act, where possible. If we can't put something right, one way that can help to move forward is seeing guilt as ***a learning point***. What can you learn from the error or misdemeanour? What will be done differently in the future? We then have a better chance of preventing it from happening again.

Either way, it might take time for our own mind to process forgiveness towards ourselves.

Important point

Guilt is an emotion to act on and not to endure.

If we dwell on any emotion or incident then we merely prolong the feelings and don't move forward. Accepting that sometimes we cannot put things right is difficult. When a situation like this happens, it is important to allow yourself to grieve, and this takes time. During this grieving process it helps considerably, if possible, to talk things through.

For a child who feels guilty, the adult needs to act as their Human to bring rationality to the situation.

It helps if the adult:

- Listens and helps the child to talk
- Checks that the emotion of guilt is an appropriate one
- Brings perspective
- Rationalises the way forward

Many children find it very consoling to know that we all do things that we might regret or feel bad about. It also helps them to know that guilt can be a useful emotion to pull us in line if we are acting out of order. However, guilt is not an emotion that is useful if it is not acted upon or is inappropriate from the start. Making amends is a very helpful way to remove feelings of guilt, along with a plan of how not to allow the situation to happen again. This way we are changing our focus from the past into the future, where we can make a difference.

Summary

- Talking helps to stabilise the mind
- Like adults, children need to express their feelings
- Talking helps to rationalise events
- Protected talking time helps to bond parents and children
- Guilt is an emotion to act upon, not to endure

Chapter 11

Habit 5 – asking for help

Both children and adults sometimes find it difficult to ask for help. However, it can be seen as a strength, particularly if we can learn when and what type of help to ask for. Asking for help is a powerful way for both adults and children to learn.

- Independence and help
- Some advantages of asking for help
- What kind of help do I need?
- Asking for help to manage the Chimp
- Troubleshooting
- Some ideas on how children learn

Independence and help

One of the features that we usually desire and encourage in children is that they learn to develop independence. Their childhood is naturally geared towards this aim, to prepare them for adulthood. It is therefore not uncommon for children to want to do things independently and most experts in the field would always encourage this. However, sometimes independence means the child misses out on learning when they can't work things out or they misinterpret something.

They can also miss out on teamwork if they don't recognise that sometimes it is far better than independent learning.

As adults, we can see that discretion needs to be used in knowing when to turn to others and when to work things out for ourselves. When we do turn to others we decide what it is that we are looking for: a sounding board, some information, some support or someone to take over. This decision-making process when asking for help is a learnt skill. Some people struggle to learn the skill of knowing what kind of help they need when it comes to problem-solving. This can lead to unhelpful behaviours, such as becoming dependent on others or being passive and not taking action.

So asking for help, as a learnt habit, has some caution attached to it. The habit is best learnt along with the skill of knowing what type of help you are asking for.

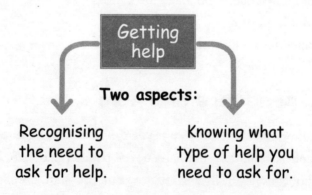

It would help a child to know *when to ask* for help and *what different types of help* are available.

Some advantages of asking for help

If a child is going to learn how to ask for help, they must believe that doing this will give them an advantage. So what beliefs will convince the child that it's sometimes good to ask for help?

Here are some suggestions:

- Trying something first is good, but it is OK to ask for help
- Wise people ask for help, because that way they can learn from others
- It isn't clever to re-discover the wheel
- Sometimes we can't do something, because we don't have the expertise
- Sometimes we can't do something, because we don't have the knowledge
- Other people can give us good ideas
- Sometimes it takes two or more people to do something
- Some mistakes are avoidable if we ask others for advice
- Sharing a task can help to remove frustration

By asking the child to discuss *their ideas* on why it might be good to ask for help, they might come up with a lot of these truths for themselves or could be guided towards them. It is better for the child to 'discover' these truths and find examples, rather than just be told them.

What kind of help do I need?

Once the child has appreciated that there are circumstances when asking for help is wise and brings advantage, then learning the skill of what *kind of help* to ask for is the next step.

Again, guiding the child to 'discover' the types of help, and also when to select each one, is the way for the child to programme their Computer system. The Computer will then advise the child automatically.

Here are some examples of types of help that we could request from someone:

- Discuss things
- Work together
- Act as a sounding board
- Show us what to do
- Mentor us
- Help with planning something
- Give some information or knowledge
- Give some support
- Give an opinion
- Offer encouragement or take an interest
- Take over

If we appreciate how each of these can help us, by thinking through examples, then we can learn how to ask for the most appropriate help.

Three steps for developing the habit of asking for help:

1 **STEP** Recognising when asking for help would be good **2** **STEP** Knowing what type of help to ask for **3** **STEP** Asking the most appropriate person

Asking for help to manage the Chimp

Managing our behaviours and emotions is a very difficult thing for all of us to do, throughout our entire lives.

It is a skill to manage your mind, and it is not an easy skill to acquire or maintain. As explained earlier, we manage our minds by letting our Human programme our Computer, which then advises the Chimp or takes over from the Chimp

by acting quickly. The child cannot do this, because they don't have fully formed Human circuitry. Therefore, they cannot programme its Computer effectively. As the carer for the child, we help to programme their Computer.

Therefore, one habit that would really help children to manage their Chimps is to ask the adult who is with them for help in doing this.

If the child can appreciate that their Chimp is hijacking them, then it would be much easier for the child to learn *the habit of asking for help when a hijack is occurring*. This would help to remove possible feelings of failure or guilt that often accompany emotional or behavioural hijacks.

In order to programme the child's Computer to ask for help early in a Chimp hijack, it would be useful to do a role-play. The role-play will give the Computer the instructions on exactly what to do if a hijack occurs.

For example, the role-play could involve the child pretending to be upset about not being able to do something, such as draw an animal, play football or tennis, have some sweets to eat or anything else that might upset them. When the child then asks for help to manage their Chimp, the adult can respond. Some suitable responses could be:

- Praise the child for asking for help with their behaviour
- Help the child to praise themselves for asking for help
- Reassure them that Chimp hijacks are normal but unhelpful
- Help the child to express their feelings and let their Chimp out, in a controlled manner!
- Offer any rational statements of reassurance
- Bring perspective to the situation
- Point to the future and better times

Example: Miranda and the spilt milk

Miranda was in high spirits, because her friend was about to arrive at the house. She had just been given some milk to drink but, instead of drinking the milk, she danced through the house with the glass in her hand. After tripping over the cat, the milk spilled across the carpet. Miranda panicked and burst into tears. Now distraught, she turns to you the adult and asks for help to manage her Chimp. How would you ideally like to respond? Notice that I said ideally!

It's probably best to begin with the outcome and ask what is the final outcome that you want? Do you want to console Miranda, punish her, let your own frustration out, ask her to learn from the incident, help her to see the consequences of her actions or even help her to see her responsibility to clean up her own mess? There is no right way to deal with this situation, only your way. What would be helpful is to think about what you want to happen and not allow your own Chimp to decide on the outcome.

Important point

Programming your own Computer in advance for inevitable events such as this will help immensely.

Miranda has asked for your help, so if your intention is to help her and see if anything can be learnt from this, then reassurance and consolation are probably the first step. It was an accident, not a deliberate act. Miranda's Chimp needs to express itself and then be brought into line with some reassuring perspective. It isn't the end of the world and everything can be put right fairly quickly.

Accidents and incidents can always be used as a good way to learn. So one possibility is to help Miranda programme into her Computer 'Whenever an accident happens, look for the solution'. The solution usually includes taking responsibility. Miranda can also learn not to dance with a glass of milk in her hand!

Troubleshooting

Some children find it difficult to ask for help. There are many reasons why this might be, so here are some of the more common ones and possible ways to respond to them.

Why won't you let me help?

Weak people ask for help.

A weakness

Believing that seeking help is a weakness is an unhelpful belief. It can be turned around by discussing this belief and giving examples and scenarios of how positive it can be to ask for help.

The replacement belief could be, 'Wise people know when to ask for help.' Sometimes children model on a hero figure. Nearly all hero figures ask for help in some way and showing this can help. For example, an elite sportsperson will ask for help from an entire team of specialist support staff: the coach, the physiotherapist, the sports psychologist and others.

Self-esteem is how you perceive yourself compared to others. Self-esteem and refusing help are sometimes connected. Occasionally, children and adults try to compensate for feelings of low self-esteem or inferiority. They can present as being wilful or arrogant. It's almost as if they are trying to conceal their own feelings about themselves and want you to see them as strong and confident. Therefore, some children try to build self-esteem by refusing to admit any weakness. Asking for help can be seen as a weakness and therefore lower their self-esteem further. To break the cycle, it helps to demonstrate what the child has accomplished or learnt, rather than put the main focus on what needs to be learnt. It can also help when children are trying to impress other children or an adult, to emphasise that praise and approval go to those who try, not just to those who accomplish. This idea of emphasising and praising a willing attitude and positive outlook can help children to feel worthy, without relying on achievement.

Fear of appearing silly

Fear of appearing silly is a very common reason why children won't attempt something or ask for help. This fear is typically based on the belief that a failure or mistake is unacceptable. The belief is that asking for help is a failure and an indication of stupidity.

Research shows that allowing errors to be made first, before finding the right way to do something, is the best way of remembering what you have learnt.[1] Errors are therefore seen as great opportunities for learning. This is a point worth endorsing with children. If a child experiences a failure with a task, they can still be resilient and bounce back. This resilience comes from the child believing that failure can be used to learn from and their intelligence is not fixed but can be improved.[2]

With trial and error learning, a key point is to follow a failed attempt at some task with immediate feedback. It seems that children learn best with immediate feedback and don't do so well if there is a delay in feeding back.[3]

One way to enhance the Computer circuits in the child's mind, so that memory can improve, is to repeat tests on learnt skills or knowledge. This is especially powerful if the child had previously learnt this by trial and error and had some failures. What we are doing neuroscientifically when we repeat successes or practise what we have learnt is to help the brain to myelinate (or speed up and strengthen) correct pathways.[4]

Important point
Making errors and then learning from these errors is a great way to learn, and often the best way to learn.

A power struggle

Occasionally parents and children get into a power struggle. (Some of you might want to challenge the word 'occasionally'!) One way to remove this struggle is for the adult to join forces with the child, by seeing whatever they are doing as a joint venture between yourself and them. By emphasising that it's a really good thing to collaborate with others, because we can share challenges and successes, the child might buy-in and also develop values for sharing.

Some ideas on how children learn

There are lots of ways in which we learn. Three main ways in which children learn are through enquiry, through solving problems, and through asking 'What if...?' questions. We will consider these in turn.

Enquiry-based learning

We have already considered the idea that children can learn more meaningfully by exploration and discovery compared to instruction. Asking for help can include helping children to pose questions.

Perhaps surprisingly, children learn from being tested for an answer, even when the answer is unknown. So the fact that they are trying to discover answers is a learning experience in its own right, even if they don't reach a conclusion.[5]

This type of learning is known as enquiry-based learning (EBL).[6]

EBL has been shown to improve language skills, vocabulary,[7] critical thinking and the ability to problem-solve.[8] By discussing a task or venture with a child they will find it easier to form questions.[9]

Problem-based learning

Learning to ask the right questions is part of problem-based learning (PBL). PBL is used a lot in many industries and organisations, including in the training of doctors.

An important point is that children are most successful when they are taught *how to learn* as well as what to learn. When taught how to learn, they develop the ability to offer clear arguments with sound reasoning. [10]

Problem-Based Learning

The foundation of PBL[11] is about helping children and young people to discover how to learn. The idea is to get groups of young people to discuss a particular problem. The adult then guides them on *how to learn to ask the right questions* to solve the problem. Once they have generated the questions, they then work as a group to answer these questions and solve the problem. The evidence is that children who learn how to form questions and answer them have an approach that is more exploratory and thoughtful than those who are taught by repetition learning.[12] [13] There is also evidence that helping children to ask relevant questions leads to them producing more thought-through designs for projects.

Many children prefer to collaborate and work in groups,

and these children learn much better when given problem-based activities.[14] [15] As children learn the need to formulate questions and are encouraged to explore, they can also be encouraged to make predictions. Learning to make predictions will activate the Human circuits in their mind and promote their development.[16]

What if...? questions

We all know that children love to ask questions, and if they are encouraged to ask some 'What if...?' questions and then try to answer them, children will invest their energies into their own learning.[17] For example, if a group of children were told that the way to bake a cake is to follow a recipe that they were given, they could be asked to question the recipe. What if... we don't put any eggs in? What if... the oven temperature is too low? What if... we add milk to the mixture? What if... we add chips to the mixture? and so on.

An alternative approach is to ask them how they would make a Sunday dinner. This will generate questions.

Group working to solve problems brings the benefits of social and interpersonal learning, but also encourages discussions and enhances understanding, even if none of the children actually starts by knowing the solution or answers.[18] There is evidence that with problem-based discussions and cooperation between children, critical thinking[19] and deeper learning is improved.

Summary

- Learning when to ask for help and what help is needed can be learnt
- Helping a child to learn to ask for help with managing their Chimp is helpful
- Recognising why a child wouldn't ask for help and then resolving this will help the child
- Basing success and praise on effort is one way to improve a child's self-esteem
- Learning from failure is a very powerful way to learn
- Discovery and investigation that are child-led have great advantages for developing the Human part of their mind

Chapter 12

Habit 6 – showing good manners

Being polite and well-mannered are habits that are usually formed early in life. This chapter looks at how we define manners and the benefits of displaying them. We will also consider how rudeness can be seen in a different light.

- Agreeing on what good manners are
- The benefits of good manners
- Answering back – an example

Agreeing on what good manners are

Our definition of good manners is a matter of personal choice, with some heavy cultural influences. An exercise that you might want to try by yourself is to consider what you think good manners are, and why you personally would want to show these towards others. What effect do you think demonstrating good manners has on you and others? This exercise in itself could help to clarify exactly why you would want to ensure that you do show good manners, and what it is that you are trying to impart to a child. The exercise could also ensure that you are a living role model! Children are very likely to imitate what they see.

Try to remember to share the explanation of why you are doing what you are doing, so that these explanations are registered in the child's Computer. When we understand the reasoning that underpins an action, the action is much more likely to be carried out and be acceptable to us.

Let's agree on what good manners are.

Children will demonstrate good manners if it makes sense for them to do so.

What are good manners?

*As a suggestion for an activity, **draw up a list with your child of what good manners are**. Children generally enjoy structure, so forming a list is a helpful way to establish desired behaviours. By* helping to draw up the list, the child will be taking ownership of the list and this makes it much more likely that the child will work with the list.

Your list of good manners will depend on what you think are good manners. Here are some examples of what many people might agree on:

- Showing appreciation with a 'thank you'
- Using the word 'please' and being polite
- Showing respect towards others and property
- Not being selfish or greedy
- Being considerate
- Putting others first
- Offering help to those in need of help
- Not offending others
- Giving compliments and not making unpleasant remarks
- Not gossiping
- Respecting cultural norms

The child could be encouraged to play a game, such as how many times they might display a specific good manner for one day. For example, how many times they are courteous to others or how many times they say 'thank you' to others.

> ### Important point
> *If a child doesn't know what good manners are, or the reason why we display good manners, then they are unlikely to demonstrate them.*

The benefits of good manners

Just as giving a gift with no strings attached makes both the giver and recipient feel good, showing good manners has a number of benefits too. Here are a few examples of the benefits:

Gratitude and improved general well-being

You could define gratitude as demonstrating an appreciation of the things that are important to you. We often overlook things and people in our lives and take them for granted. By stopping to appreciate what we have and who we have in our lives, we can gain a sense of gratefulness. By expressing gratitude, such as thanking others, we can be seen as polite and well mannered.

Simple acts of gratitude can have significant consequences in terms of our general well-being.[1] There is evidence that helping a child to focus on the good things in their life can have emotional and interpersonal benefits, if they do this with a sense of gratefulness. [2]

When I stop and think about it, there is so much I am grateful for.

As adults, we experience a more positive perception of a partner when we express gratitude. This is also true with friendships. A consequence of this is that where gratitude is shown, partners and friends are more able to be frank about any relationship concerns.[3] When we show gratitude towards someone, it makes them feel respected and valued and they are more likely to help us.[4]

Important point
Expressing gratitude can strengthen relationships.

Improved confidence

Good manners can bring confidence. In many social settings, children have no knowledge of how to act. By giving the child *a set of learnt behaviours*, such as manners for particular circumstances, the child will have a set of behaviours to fall back on. Routines will give the child some sense of security, especially if their behaviour results in approval, which is perceived as a positive outcome.

Avoiding distress

By being considerate to others we show respect, whereas rude behaviour shows disrespect and can damage relationships. Rude behaviour has been shown to later produce anxiety, sorrow and pain in the person being rude.[5] Children who are rude often do so because they are being defensive and lack confidence. This rudeness can be rewired by positive learning experiences.[6] One function of the Chimp, especially the orbitofrontal area, is to make sure everyone accepts us.[7] Distress is not unusual if we think we are being criticised or rejected. Therefore, positive feedback on any helpful behaviour will strongly encourage this helpful behaviour to be repeated.

Sometimes, children showing a lack of manners appear to be rude because they have not practised the habit of displaying good manners and are caught off-guard. They do not want to be rude.

Answering back – an example

Marcus's parents are being driven to distraction because Marcus cannot stop answering back. Despite telling him that it is rude to answer back, he still continues to do it. They are concerned that he will continue doing this as he enters adult life and this will be unpleasant for all of those around him and do him no favours. What could they do? Here is an offer of a solution for approaching this.

We could look at four separate parts to the solution:

1. Marcus needs to be operating with the same understanding as the adult speaking with him
2. Marcus needs to accept that he has a Chimp that will always react quickly
3. The adult needs to accept that Marcus has a Chimp and not react and go into Chimp mode themselves
4. The adult could instil a Computer programme into Marcus for when a challenge happens

1 – The same understanding

In order to explain this idea, I am going to challenge what we mean by answering back. I will give an exaggerated example to bring the point to life.

Imagine a scenario where you are at work and one of your senior managers announces that, from now on, your hours of work will be changed. There is no discussion and you will be expected to do hours that are really inconvenient to you. Not impossible, but definitely inconvenient. When you try to ask about the reasoning, or to see if there is any negotiation around this, you are abruptly told to stop answering back and to get on with it. To add to this, you are told not to mention it again and that if you do, this will be seen as rude and insolent and there will be consequences. Pretty unpleasant!

What you would want to do is to understand the situation and in the end accept it, provided it is reasonable, even if you might not agree. This is your employer, after all, and they pay your wages! If their reasoning is sound and legal, although not pleasant, then the hours might have to change. What you wouldn't expect is to be given no explanation, or a warning or threat, which stops you from expressing your feelings or ideas.

At the same time, what the employer wouldn't want, if they were being reasonable and allowing you to question the decision, is some abusive, aggressive or rude approach from you when you do respond. Therefore, what you are likely to do is to be assertive and ask if you could understand their reasoning and then discuss this. Marcus is trying to do the same, but he hasn't got the skills.

If your employer took the time to sit down and explain why they have to make some decisions that you might not like or agree with, you might feel differently about the situation. Now that you have an explanation and you can understand what your employer is saying, you are both operating with the same understanding. This means that you can appreciate why you are being asked to agree to change your hours.

There is little difference between this scenario and a child being told what to do, without explanation or being able to discuss the situation.

2 – The Chimp reacts quickly

Even though you have the explanation for your change of hours, your Chimp might still try and react rather than allowing you, the Human and Computer, to use your interpersonal skills to discuss the situation and see if there is a compromise. As adults, we tend not to react because we have developed some measure of interpersonal skills, which mainly operate via our Computer. We have learnt how to respond appropriately.

Teenagers and young children are on a steep learning curve. This is not just about facts and methods; it is also about reasoning and interpersonal skills. Even if the child understands what you are saying, they are unlikely to have the interpersonal skills to then discuss this in an adult and polite manner. Instead, their Chimp will react and is likely to present the child as being rude, challenging and disobedient. What the child is really trying to do is to understand your reasoning and values.

The reasoning is about appreciating why you are saying what you are saying and what consequences there will be. They are also learning about values, which can be in the form of manners. Answering back could therefore be understood as a very crude way for the child, who has poor interpersonal skills and poor Chimp management, to try and understand your stance. The answering back is the Chimp taking over with a fast and probably rude reply.

3 – Acceptance with dignity!

Many parents tell me how they go totally Chimp themselves when their child's Chimp prods them with constant answering back. This can lead to a loss of dignity, and on reflection, they realise that this is not the best response.

It can help if you can see answering back in a different light. It is the child's way of learning. They don't intend to be rude. *They just don't have the interpersonal skills to silence their Chimp and allow their Human to respond in a tactful and appropriate way*. If you can accept these points, then it is less likely that your own Chimp will react with an equally unreasonable and rude response, and this might help you to retain your own dignity!

4 – The way forward

How could you move forward with your child to get a better outcome when they have a natural Chimp outburst? You could work with your child to instil a Computer programme for when a challenge happens.

Here are some suggestions that might help you to do this. First remember that we are all prone to react quickly via our Chimp to anything that doesn't please us. It is so important for you not to muddle your child up with their Chimp and also not to muddle yourself up with your own Chimp.

Begin with the outcome that you would like to happen. Most people will probably say:

• I would like my child to understand why I am asking them to do something or to accept something that they will not find pleasant
• I would also like to be calm and in a good place myself throughout the entire interaction

If we begin with this premise, then the starting point is to make sure that you are in a good place and well prepared before the incident takes place. This way, your Chimp won't get involved because the Computer within you will respond with a programmed response to manage your own emotions.

To get into a good place, try asking yourself what you would expect a normal, healthy Chimp to do when it is told to do something it doesn't want to do? So, if there is an outburst from the child's Chimp, remain calm and celebrate this as normal and healthy! This is a choice that you can make: celebrate or get annoyed.

If you have decided that your child's behaviour is therefore normal and healthy, *but not acceptable*, you will have a basis for *discussing this with the child*.

It might be worth putting other facts into your Computer to help you to remain in Human mode. Here are some suggestions:

- When the child's Chimp reacts, it will be a learning opportunity for the child
- Some children need to know what isn't acceptable before they understand what is acceptable
- Most children go through a rebellious stage – this doesn't last forever
- This is a chance for the child to learn to manage their own Chimp
- This is an opportunity for you to learn to manage your Chimp!

The second part of the plan is to discuss the situation with the child. Clearly, this is best done when the child is quiet and in a receptive state. It is best to try and have these discussion *before any incident happens* rather than during.

The child needs to understand that their Chimp is likely to hijack them when it hears something unpleasant, especially an instruction or request from the person in charge. This reaction is probably going to involve their Chimp speaking and reacting in a way that is not demonstrating good interpersonal skills. In other words, the child needs to appreciate that poor reactions from their Chimp won't help them to get a good response from the person being 'attacked'.

The discussion could include explaining what is acceptable as a response. The child needs to know *what they can do* when they can't have what they want. So for example, they could ask you for help to manage their Chimp and talk to it. Discussions could also include exactly what are *helpful interpersonal skills*, and how asking about, or challenging, conflicting instructions in a constructive way is one worth learning. This way you are much more likely to get a constructive discussion to take place, and a better outcome.

How can you achieve a really good response from the child's Computer rather than their Chimp? One method, which most children like, is to role-play some different scenarios.

You could always choose the ones that you know are likely to occur for your particular child. It will probably help you to choose the ones that are also likely to get your own Chimp out. Here are some suggestions:

- Getting ready for school
- Eating food that they don't like
- Stopping play when a meal is ready
- Getting homework done

For each scenario, try to first explain to the child why the request is being made and the effects it has if it is not carried out. Then try to help the child to form a plan for their Computer to carry out, in order to prevent their Chimp from taking over and doing something that they will later regret. Then act the scenario out and, if the child manages, praise them generously. Seeing an instruction as a game that needs carrying out might result in the child's Chimp actually joining in so that it can win and receive the praise.

Summary

- Agreeing on what good manners are helps a child to take ownership
- If a child understands the reasoning behind good manners, they are much more likely to display them
- Good manners can bring well-being, confidence and improved relationships
- Chimps don't do manners, only Humans can, and the Computer carries them out
- Try not to muddle your child up with their Chimp when it comes to displaying manners

Chapter 13

Habit 7 – trying new things

Trying new things can enrich a child and improve their physical and psychological health. It is always worth considering what your real aim is when helping your child to try new things, and what you measure as success.

- Why do you want your child to try new things?
- Thoughts on independence
- Potential barriers for the child when trying new activities

Why do you want your child to try new things?

That might seem an odd question, but it's worth answering. Trying new things has self-evident benefits, but often the real reason for encouraging children to try new things can become lost in the drive to help them to accomplish something. For example, a parent might want their child to build self-confidence. To do this, they decide to help the child to read out loud. However, they then get side-tracked into making sure that the child can read aloud and forget that the real reason for doing this is to help build self-confidence. If the child doesn't manage to read aloud very well, then they might end up with less self-confidence. One way around this is to let the child know that as long as they have a go at reading out loud, then you see this as success. Reading aloud then becomes a very welcome bonus but being *applauded for trying* builds the self-confidence.

Too often in sport, we see parents who encourage their child to participate in order to learn such things as how to work in a team, organise their time or relate to others. These aims are then forgotten and winning or achieving becomes the new goal.

Even trying new food can become a battle. Parents have said to me that they want their child to be healthy by eating the right things. The battle that ensues often creates immense stress in the child, and also in the parent. Psychological health then takes second place to winning a battle about food. I accept that it is important to eat well, so the example that follows looks at how we might do this.

Peter and the new food

Peter has reached the age of eight and his diet has slowly narrowed and become unacceptable to his father. His father decides to try and get Peter to eat some vegetables. Let battle commence!

Peter's father places the vegetables in front of Peter and encourages his son to see if he likes them. Now let's get real here: not many people would put sprouts, cabbage, broccoli or carrots in front of burgers, chocolate, doughnuts or chips. So the chance of success is probably low.

What could the father do to increase the chance of success? Please note that I said increase the chance, not get Peter to be an avid fan of sprouts.

If you ask yourself why some adults have a balanced diet and why they want their children to follow them, then the answers could give the clues to aid success. Some key knowledge that influences adults could include:

- We understand that balanced diets are good for us
- We focus on particular foods because we know exactly what they offer for health. For example, onions aid a healthy skin and spinach has a lot of iron in it
- We accept that eating certain foods is an acquired taste
- We recognise the consequences of not eating some roughage
- We recognise the need for vitamins

In other words, our choice of food is based on sound reasoning and not just immediate gratification. Our Chimp eats impulsively and for pleasure, whereas our Human eats by considering the consequences of what we eat.

If a child understands and believes the advantages of eating a varied diet, they are much more likely to try new foods. Therefore, it might help if children find out for themselves what they would gain from trying new foods and establish these beliefs in their Computer. This will then advise the Chimp. Well at least that's the theory!

Here are some practical ideas on how you might improve the chances of new foods being tried:

- Encouraging the child to discover some facts around certain foods. For example, spinach is loaded with iron that helps form red blood cells, which carry oxygen to muscles to give us more energy and strength. This can appeal to some children to try spinach, as they will then relate spinach to strength

- Explain to the child that foods are for healthy growth. For example: helping them to grow taller and fitter, developing their brain for thinking and strength for playing sports

- Growing their own food, such as vegetables, and then sharing these with a parent can break the taboo around trying vegetables, especially if the child helps to prepare the vegetables for eating

- It can be helpful to a child if we explain that when trying new foods it can take some time before we come to appreciate the taste or texture. The child can then understand that instant pleasure from a mouthful of vegetables is unlikely to happen!

- Mixing new foods with favourite foods can also work!
- You could ask the child to become the 'food police'

The food police officers

One family were struggling to get their three children to eat almost any healthy food put before them. I asked the parents to try a game whereby the children became the 'food police officers'. Their role was to take over the responsibility for the health of the family by ensuring that everyone ate a varied and healthy diet.

Sometimes, when children or young adults are given a responsibility for something, they become ardent devotees to the cause. These children took this very seriously and even had police caps bought for them. They loved monitoring to see that everyone ate well, including the children. Ironically, it was the father who wanted some relief from the stringency!

Important point

To help children to take something seriously, offer to give them responsibility for doing it.

Thoughts on independence

Trying new things and testing children's limits can help children to develop confidence, independence and autonomy, provided some simple guidelines are followed. Research often states what might be considered as obvious, but the obvious is not always put into practice! Encouraging children to try new things can be helpful, provided the carer is not over protective or disapproving of independence. Young children who experience disapproval of any form of independence can become inhibited and see independence as wrong.[1] The difficulty is that independence can be learnt in two ways: socially acceptable and socially unacceptable. Socially acceptable ways of learning independence mean that the way in which they are learning is constructive to the child and also to those around them. Socially unacceptable ways of learning independence mean that the child might be learning, but it is causing distress or harm to those nearby.

For example, suppose a child is trying to learn how a toy works. Their older sister, who knows how it works, is watching.

If the child allows the sister to watch and give them occasional guidance, then the child is learning to be independent and not reliant on the sister. All is well. However, if the child refuses to let the sister watch or becomes hostile or aggressive if she tries to offer guidance, then their interaction becomes unacceptable. Constructive independent learning is achieved by being respectful to those nearby.

Learning how independence can be seen as socially acceptable will help the child to develop their own initiative. However, if the child does not appreciate how to develop independence in a socially acceptable way then conflict or guilt is likely to arise.[2]

It would be helpful to explain these points to a young child so that they understand how to see and develop independence in a psychologically constructive way.

Important point
Encourage independence in a socially acceptable way.

It is not always easy for the adult to avoid directly criticising a child, especially if the child is acting in an unhelpful way. Sometimes letting the child know what would be helpful can turn this around. For example, the adult could explain that when we are working independently, we ought to consider the effects on others close by. It might help to suggest that accepting some guidance is good and this builds friendships. If the child wants to try something for themselves, then teaching them to ask politely, rather than impulsively taking over, can help immensely.

Let's talk about how we can get along with others, as we learn.

These points are always worth discussing with the child before the child has begun to try something new. It is much harder to manage a conflict situation than it is to prevent it from occurring in the first place.

Potential barriers for the child when trying new activities

Trying new activities can be stressful and testing to many children. For the rest of this chapter we will consider some potential barriers and ways to avoid them. These barriers can be very important to address, as many of the following unhelpful habits and beliefs that originate in childhood can be carried into adulthood.

We will consider:

- Low confidence and fear of failure
- Low self-esteem
- Perfectionism
- Excessive worrying

Low confidence and fear of failure

When children are asked to try out an unfamiliar activity that involves potential failure, many refuse to engage because of the fear of failure. A fear of not being able to do or achieve something is usually based on worries about possible comments and opinions of others.

Imagine for the moment that you live on a desert island all alone. Do you think that you would fear failure in anything that didn't have dire consequences? If no one was about to know the result or the outcome, would you be afraid to try?

I have had the privilege of working at medical school, teaching future doctors. They take many exams and each year I would see, as a regular problem, some very stressed students with a fear of failure. Whenever I have asked the students to imagine living on a desert island or even just to imagine that no one else saw the result of the exam, even if they had multiple attempts before passing it, how would they feel? The answer is nearly always that they wouldn't be bothered then about the result. In other words, they are basing their fear on what others think.

Some students would say that their fear of failure was

based on the consequences of failing, such as not becoming a doctor. I can appreciate this. However, this fear is not of the consequences but rather of the fear of not being able to cope with the consequences, which is a very different thing. As adults there is very little that we cannot deal with. Our Chimp brain is fooling us into believing that any failure means that life can't go on. We can't recover from a failure – everyone has seen it and now has a low opinion of us.

As adults, we can challenge all of this. A child cannot challenge these beliefs. This is because the child's immature brain looks to an adult for security and approval. The adult must effectively again become the Human in the child's head. How do we do this?

This will depend on your own beliefs and values. Only you can decide how you want to approach a child who lacks confidence or struggles with a failure. Here is a suggestion. The two aspects that the adult Human part of the mind brings to a failure or setback are:

- Perspective
- Values

Perspective means explaining to the child that this isn't the end of the world and we can redeem most things. It also means that we can deal with a failure or something we can't redeem.

Values mean that we decide how important something is to us. Not just the success but also how important other people's opinions of us should be. For a child, the opinion of the parent or carer is paramount. Values also include whether you think trying is more important than succeeding. The Chimp bases its value on what it has and what it can achieve. The Human bases its value on who they are and how they approach life: doing your best therefore becomes the measure of success.

Of course it's good to applaud achievement, but is it more important than applauding effort?

Is it good that I did my best?

Important point

Every child can gain applause for their efforts and feel good about themselves. Not every child can achieve everything they want to.

Fear of failure is often based on the false belief that, when we try something, we can always manage to *achieve* our best. This is obviously unrealistic. Nobody can always manage to achieve their best, even when giving their best effort. If we can programme the Computer with the truths that '*giving your best effort is all that you can do*', and '*achieving your best on the day is all that you can try for and hope that it happens*', then the concept of failure is given a reality check. We can't guarantee success, but we can guarantee best effort. 'Giving your best' obviously means exactly that: full effort. The outcome of that effort is then something we have to accept. Of course we all want successful outcomes and 'failures' are disappointing. However, as adults we are big enough to manage an unsuccessful outcome and the disappointment. Children need support and approval to accept a 'failure'. Again, as stated earlier, failure can be interpreted as a learning point.

Self-esteem

Children are trying to build self-esteem. As stated in the previous paragraph, the Chimp will try and build this on what they can achieve. There is nothing wrong with this, but there are some points to consider.

The Chimp believes that when it has achieved its goals, whatever they might be, it will be happy and have high self-esteem. The problem is that the Chimp is never satisfied for long and will soon dismiss any achievements it has made and start again from a point of low self-esteem. The reason it dismisses great achievements is that the Chimp also uses achievement to be accepted by others. It sees being accepted by others as extremely important, and therefore it cannot get it wrong. So it challenges anything it has achieved and doubts what it has achieved is good enough. This usually results in the child being very critical of themselves and what they have achieved. Any achievements are therefore doubted as not being good enough and need to be constantly improved upon in order to gain acceptance. If the child is allowed to be in Chimp mode and uses achievement for building self-esteem and proving their worth, then the consequence is usually unhelpful. It can lead to negative emotions and a sense of always having to keep proving themselves by further achievement.

The Human builds self-esteem and acceptance on values but can also enjoy achievement. The Human therefore works on self-respect. Self-respect and working with values gives the human good self-esteem. The Human can drive for achievement, while recognising that achievement is something to be proud of but not base self-esteem on. Self-esteem is based on respecting and loving the type of person that you are.

| My self-esteem is based on what I can achieve. | My self-esteem is based on my values and self-respect. |

Perfectionism

The Chimp brain and the Human brain have different outlooks and understanding of what perfection means. If they can work together, then the outcome will be optimal. I will cover this in very black-and-white terms to try and make things simple, but clearly there will be shades of grey.

The Human sees perfection as '*doing the best I can*'. This means putting *maximum effort* into a task and trying your best. The Human accepts that we don't usually achieve what we are capable of, because of factors that are often outside our control. For example, running a 100-metre sprint seems very straightforward. However, on the day, no matter how much an athlete tries, there will be variable performance. This could be due to many factors, both physiological and psychological. Their body and mind are not fully under their control, and this is why we watch the 100-metre race! If an athlete got the same perfect run every time then we wouldn't watch, because it would become predictable.

The Human therefore aims for perfection, but knows that once we have given everything, we have to accept that we don't often get perfection.

The Chimp, on the other hand, is unforgiving and demands that we achieve perfection. It cannot accept less than perfection, because this is what it wants and this part of the brain does not work with reality. If we allow ourselves to accept our Chimp's view of the world and perfection in particular, then we can expect to feel frustrated, angry, upset or whatever other emotion that taking this approach will inevitably evoke.

The way that the two can work together is to switch over once the work is done. So by all means set off in Chimp mode, which will demand perfection and provide the enormous drive to reach perfection. The Human brain will join in with this. However, once you have finished what you are doing, it is time to switch to Human mode and accept that you couldn't have done any more, if you gave your best. Now we might experience elation or disappointment, but we can be proud of doing our best.

Working together

An adult can accept disappointment and use this next time to improve things, if possible. The adult can do this because inside their Computer they have a simple belief that they can deal with anything that life throws at them, including disappointments. Children, on the other hand, cannot do this because they don't usually believe that they can deal with anything in life. This is reasonable because children cannot lead an independent life. Therefore, the adult accompanying a child must again become the Human and Computer to the child.

Excessive worrying

Children are in a very vulnerable and necessarily dependent position. Therefore, it seems very natural that their Chimp will worry about most things. If the child can be encouraged to understand that their Chimp is doing a good job by worrying, then this will help to normalise the experience for them. Although it's normal to worry, it isn't helpful. If the child can be taught how to diffuse the worry and turn it into an action, then this will make the worry potentially very constructive.

What could the child do with worry? First accept that *it is normal*, even if it is not pleasant. Learning to *talk about their worries* is the first and most important step to settling down the Chimp. Adults use their Human and their beliefs within the Computer to settle down their Chimp. One belief that both adults and children can programme into their Computer is that, when the Chimp starts to worry, it is *a message from the Chimp to act*. *Finding a solution* to any problem rather than focusing on it will help. Getting things into *perspective* is another big help. Most children's Chimps are constantly on high alert for danger, particularly when it comes to security or possible criticism. Reassurance, encouragement and praise can go a long way to settling worries.

Summary

- Try to clarify your own reasons for helping a child to try new things
- If children understand why they are trying new things they are more likely to do them

- Giving children responsibility for learning helps build autonomy
- Encourage independence in a socially acceptable way
- Removing barriers to trying new things involves the adult acting as the Human and Computer for the child
- Removing unhelpful habits during childhood prevents them from being carried into adult life

Chapter 14

Habit 8 – accepting that 'no' means 'no'!

It's inevitable that we will all have times when we don't want to accept 'no' for an answer. This usually results in a Chimp hijack. As adults, we learn to programme our Computers to deal with this. Children need help to programme their Computer in order to manage disappointment.

- Helping to programme the child's Computer
- Helpful beliefs
- An action plan
- Overreacting
- Seeing the child beyond the Chimp

Helping to programme the child's Computer

It is natural and healthy for a child, or an adult, to react when they can't have what they want or when things don't go the way that they want them to. However, reacting isn't usually helpful.

By going back to basics, we can see how to minimise the child's reaction and also how to avoid the conflict that can result from a child not getting their own way.

The child's mind works the same as the adult's. Therefore, the first reaction we expect to see will be from the Chimp. To move forward, we need to not engage with the Chimp but to rely on the child having a well-programmed Computer.

Important point

The Computer must be programmed before the event.

Let's start with two scenarios:

Carl and bedtime

Carl knows that his bedtime is at 8 p.m. However, every night he tries to stay up for longer. Every night there is the same battle. Sometimes, because he has behaved well and it's the weekend, he is allowed to stay up until 8.30 or 9.00 p.m. The bedtime battle is driving his parent up the wall. The parent can't understand why Carl just can't accept the rules and go to bed peacefully. When Carl is confronted, he just rolls around the floor and the parent's Chimp takes over.

Denise and the tattoo

Denise is angry and upset with her parents because they will not let her get a tattoo. Two of her friends have got tattoos on their ankles and she feels it is unfair that her parents are being unreasonable. Denise cannot take 'no' for an answer and brings up the topic regularly. Her inability to accept 'no' is causing stress to her parents.

Helpful beliefs

As a starting point, we could ask what beliefs we want to establish, that will help a child to accept that sometimes 'no' really does mean 'no'?

If we consider how most adults programme their own Computer to accept that things might not go their way, then this will give us some ideas. There are several beliefs that might be in the adult's Computer that could stop the adult's Chimp in its tracks. Here are some possible examples:

- Life is not always fair
- Sometimes we have to accept that we can't have what we want
- Sometimes we have to be patient and wait for something
- Complaining and getting upset doesn't help
- Accepting the unchangeable is sensible
- Working with a fixed situation is better than being frustrated by it
- Moving on to something else is helpful
- Having a plan to deal with disappointment makes things easier

Imagine *you* are trying to deal with a situation in which you can't have your own way. What beliefs are you holding that would help you to deal with the situation and get over it? Could you share these with your child?

If you act as a role model to show how you also have to manage yourself when you can't have what you want, the child might copy your behaviour.

An action plan

Having helpful beliefs in the Computer will settle the Chimp down. However, if we don't have a plan to move forward, it is very likely the Chimp will still come back complaining. This is why, when Carl's parent confronted him, Carl didn't have a plan and so began to roll about on the floor. By helping the child to appreciate that we need to have *a plan to move on*, they can learn this as a habit for life.

Therefore, there are two ways to help the child to accept what they feel is unacceptable:

- Programme the Computer with helpful beliefs
- Programme the Computer with a plan to move on – an action plan

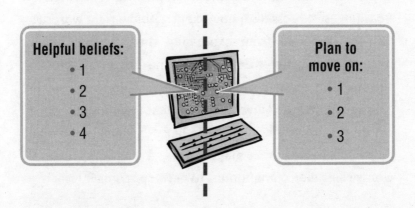

Important point

Having an action plan ready to deal with any disappointment or frustration is very constructive and can save hours of agitation!

The stages of an action plan

Here is a suggested action plan for when a disappointment takes place and the child has to accept that 'no' really does mean 'no'.

Step 1

Accept that disappointment or frustration is a very healthy and normal reaction.

It would help to discuss this with your child and to help them to appreciate that healthy reactions are sometimes unhelpful. However, accepting that it is normal to feel this way, such as being angry, frustrated or sad, can be reassuring and remove any possible guilt.

Step 2

Express any emotional reaction and feelings constructively.

Learning to express disappointment with the right words can prevent someone from expressing their disappointment inappropriately. So even a simple and obvious expression such as 'This really disappoints me' can help to release the emotional pressure valve! It's important to choose the 'right' words, because saying something like, 'This makes me really angry', might only make matters worse. Using very emotional words can cause our emotions to become stronger.[1]

> ## Important point
> It is helpful for the child to use the right words to express themselves; for example, saying I am 'disappointed' is usually better than saying I am 'angry'.

Step 3
Form a plan for going forward.
Any difficult situation that doesn't seem to have a way forward is likely to be a source of trouble. It is important to find a way forward whenever a problem arises. Seeing a way forward with a plan helps us all to move on. For example, putting a new challenge in place could be a way to get over a 'failure'. Another example would be to use a distraction, such as a pleasurable activity to effectively change the focus of the child.

We can now review the two scenarios from the start of this chapter to see these steps in action.

Carl and bedtime reviewed
One possible reason for a collision between parents and children is because they do not have the same understanding of a situation when starting a conversation. So in this example, we could ask the parent what is in their mind when they ask Carl to go to bed at eight?

The answer could be that Carl becomes very tired and grumpy if he doesn't get his sleep, or there might be many other reasons why his parent wants him to go to bed at eight: Does Carl understand the benefits to him if he goes to bed at eight, or the consequences if he stays up beyond eight? Sometimes discussing with a child the reasoning behind a 'no means no' answer can help immensely. However, this has to be done BEFORE the event occurs, because once the battle is on, Carl will remain in Chimp mode and is not likely ***to be able to*** listen, reason or discuss. Therefore, if you were going to try and reason with Carl, it would need to be done when he is in a sensible and receptive mode, well before bedtime. If you can talk through the benefits of going to bed and the consequences of him staying up, then he might register these in his Computer when it comes to bedtime.

If the actual act of going to bed has no positives, why would we expect Carl to want to comply? Is it possible that getting into bed could have its own rewards? This would then be the plan to move him away from the desire to stay up. Examples include:

- Some children willingly go to bed if there is a bedtime story. There is evidence that this also helps them to sleep better[2]
- Others will go if they are given a star on a star chart for getting to bed on time. This can then be traded in for a reward each week
- Some children love to talk through their day, and bedtime is an ideal way to end the day and plan the next day. This special, sacrosanct time can make for good parent-child bonding

Important point

If a child can discuss and have ownership of the 'rules' of bedtime, then they are much more likely to comply with them.

What about the concession of staying up late on Saturday nights? As long as this is discussed with reasoning beforehand, most children will appreciate the different bedtime from a weeknight.

There is a danger! Remember the 'variable success' principle from Chapter 4. If we have intermittent reinforcement then we can strengthen unwanted behaviours. What this means is that, if we are inconsistent and give way at times, the behaviour we don't want is likely to become stronger. So, let's say Carl has been good and we allow him to stay up late during the week. Carl has been taught that there is always a possibility that he could stay up late, if he can convince us. Therefore, he will always keep trying and pleading because he has discovered that there are exceptions. The important point is to be consistent with the bedtime both during the week *and* at weekends.

Important point

Try to be consistent in your approach. Inconsistent approaches will encourage the child to challenge you.

Denise and the tattoo reviewed

This scenario is typical of many situations where a parent is making a decision that is based on an opinion. These parents don't feel it is right for a young person to have a tattoo; other parents might disagree. In order to try and resolve the conflict, it could help to go through the steps outlined above.

First the parents could express an understanding of the emotions that Denise is feeling and agree that it is reasonable for her to have these emotions. This demonstration of understanding is often very helpful for the child.

The second step is to help her to express how she feels in a constructive way. Allowing her to speak and gather her thoughts will help her to release some of these emotions.

The third step, moving forward with a plan, is best done by discussion, where possible! Discussions about people regretting getting certain tattoos, or changing what tattoo they have, will probably fall on deaf ears. Rationality often fails with an emotionally distressed young person, so sometimes speaking about emotions instead can help. For example, expressing as a parent how much you don't want her to make a mistake, and how much this would distress you, is more likely to be heard than logical reasons, letting her know that you might be making a mistake but you have to go with your feelings. Following emotional discussions, it is helpful to try and encourage rationalisation of the situation. Eventually, Denise will have the right to make her own decisions. Therefore, eventually, she might have the tattoo she wants. Offering a series of temporary tattoos in the meantime might help!

Overreacting

When a child can't have what they want or becomes distressed, their Chimp usually overreacts to the situation. A child's Chimp *naturally* overreacts. This part of the mind does not have the ability to gain a sense of perspective. Therefore it has a tendency to see everything catastrophically. Some adults who show this overreaction to setbacks have learnt this behaviour in childhood and repeat the behaviour throughout adult life, instead of stopping and reconsidering how their Chimp can be managed.

Important point
It is a very healthy Chimp that overreacts.

Managing the Chimp, and preventing overreactions from occurring, means turning to the Computer again. We can first programme the Computer to *recognise* when an overreaction is taking place. Then *accept* that the overreaction is happening and turn the emotions *into words* by expressing what that overreaction is about: this will help to clarify concerns and fears. Finally, we can bring some perspective into the picture by looking at what this situation will mean in a few hours, a few weeks or even a year's time; this usually helps a lot. This is not an easy process for an adult to do, let alone a child. So it is fair to say that the adult will need to take the lead until the child develops the habit of checking any overreactions.

Some suggested steps to prevent an overreaction from persisting

- Learn to recognise that an overreaction is taking place
- Express in words what the overreaction is about
- Bring perspective by considering if the issue will be important in the future

Seeing the child beyond the Chimp

We have discussed in detail how the mind is a machine that can hijack you and have its own agenda. If you can view a lot of your child's actions as being a hijack, then you might not only feel differently towards events but are also likely to respond differently. Within the model, we can see that the child will operate from the Chimp system for much of the time. So they are likely to be impulsive, not think through consequences and follow natural instincts. If you can see this happening and recognise that it is only the Chimp within the child hijacking them, then your approach can be modified. You could now join forces with the child to help them to recognise what is happening and then help them to manage their Chimp. The Human within the child will welcome this, just as adults who are hijacked also welcome support to manage their Chimp.

Example: the five-year-old's temper tantrum

Joey has tried to win a game when playing on his iPad. He has failed and can't accept this. He reacts by throwing the iPad at the floor and starts screaming.

Before we look at how you might want to manage this situation, let's step back and see what the neuroscience of the mind is telling us is actually happening.

The Chimp within the child is likely to see failure in the game as catastrophic and it is likely to believe that others will perceive them as being stupid and a failure as a person. The Human within the child is disappointed at not winning and is most likely embarrassed by the reaction of the Chimp and doesn't want to get into trouble. The Computer is very likely to be blank! The rules of the mind dictate that the Chimp is strongest and can only realistically be managed via the Computer. Therefore, with this situation the child is fated to act in a destructive way.

A way forward

We can pre-programme the Computer by discussing with the child what might happen if their Chimp gets out. As we have seen earlier, a simple way to do this is to practise with the child. Help them to have fun by role-playing a temper tantrum by their Chimp. By *discussing* how the child would like to react to a failure, the child will have *ownership* of the Computer's plan to manage their Chimp.

For example, you and your child could come up with something like this for a Computer programme to manage failure:

- *Let the Chimp express itself in a helpful way*. This could be by letting the child tell you exactly how their Chimp is feeling. Alternatively, it could be more physical. For example, by letting their Chimp do something simple such as jump up and down five times. Some children will not be so energetic and might want to let their Chimp have a quiet rant. As we are all unique, only you and your child can establish what will work for both of you. It helps immensely if the child has ownership of the plan.

- *Say sorry*, if the Chimp has caused any problems by its actions.

- *Try to put right any problems*, if there are practical things that can be done. You might need to suggest to the child what could be done, such as pick up the iPad and place it somewhere safe.

- If possible and appropriate, encourage the child to *have a laugh at their Chimp's antics*.

- *Ask what they can learn from this?* For example, this could be about perspective or about doing your best and accepting that things don't always work out.

What we are effectively doing is giving the child a plan to work with that the Computer can put straight into action and make into a habit.

We could also put into the child's Computer some truths and values that the Chimp will see when it turns to the Computer. You would have to decide what these truths are, as we all have different views. Here are some examples that you may or may not agree with:

- Games are about fun
- Enjoying the game is as important as winning
- The outcome of a game doesn't define me
- People like good losers
- I can't be good at everything
- Things don't always go the way I want them to
- Humans get disappointed, but Chimps get angry or upset

These values and truths might need to be reinforced many times before the child can use them effectively. This principle is no different for adults. It's worth sitting down with your child and working together on these beliefs or values for various situations.

Beliefs usually underpin a Chimp reaction. In this case, Joey's Computer had been programmed by his Chimp to believe that, if you can't win, everybody sees you as a failure. It can be very enlightening to see what beliefs a child holds, as these beliefs will often dictate their reaction or behaviours.

Summary

- Children need help to constructively programme their Computer
- To programme a Computer effectively it needs:
  - Helpful beliefs
  - An action plan
- Helping children to use the right words to express how they feel can diffuse unhelpful emotions
- Giving a child ownership of agreed behaviours makes them likelier to see them happen
- Try to be consistent in your approach and behaviours
- Try to see the child beyond the Chimp

Chapter 15

Habit 9 – learning to share

Sharing is a very useful habit to acquire, as it helps to establish and maintain friendships, aids learning, improves interpersonal skills and promotes collaboration.

- What are the advantages of sharing?
- Sharing through practical projects
- Sharing experiences and teamwork
- Troubleshooting
- Some ideas on prevention and management of conflict

What are the advantages of sharing?

Although, to many children the idea of sharing things with other children is difficult to accept, there are many advantages to sharing. We will cover the topic of sharing in the first part of this chapter and then go on to some related topics about learning. Finally, after the theory, we can look at the reality and do some troubleshooting!

Altruism

Being altruistic and sharing has a beneficial effect on most people. Giving a present can do as much for us as receiving a present, as we experience the joy of giving.[1] Helping others, likewise, gives a sense of well-being and often demonstrates our values in action. One way of sharing is to engage in an altruistic project to help others. We will discuss projects in greater detail later in this chapter, as they can have multiple beneficial effects on children.

Making friends

Children between the ages of nine and eleven begin to place great importance on friendships and peer relationships, which increase in strength and complexity.[2] This results in a move away from family and parents and can bring some worries about being accepted and popular with peers.[3]

If we look at the developmental stages in children, we can see that they start from a position of total dependence on an adult and then move through stages towards independence. Therefore, as the child grows towards adolescence, most begin to look to their peers for support rather than an adult. During the teenage years, when peer pressure is at its peak, the peer group typically becomes immensely significant to their emotional stability and resilience. As teenagers progress into adulthood, the peer group becomes more of a guide than a basis for stability.

Building peer relationships is therefore an important skill to acquire. Helping a child to become more resilient later in life begins during childhood. Children who react with strong emotions tend to create negative feedback from their peers. By helping a child to manage their emotions, they can elicit more positive responses from their peers, which helps to develop resilience later in life.[4]

It is at a young age that children learn to accept different points of view and to share ideas. *Having a discussion about this can help children to focus on what sharing is about and how friendships are formed on values*. It is important that a child understands what values are; these are the behaviours we want to demonstrate based on our morals and ethics.

Sharing promotes friendship

The older I get the more important friends become.

Important point
A major aspect of learning to share is about implementing values, such as respect, selflessness and consideration of others.

Sharing through practical projects

Children usually have difficulty seeing the advantages of sharing. Talking about the advantages doesn't usually bring them to life. The best way to make the advantages apparent is to help the child to experience them first hand.

Research has indicated that when children have a hands-on learning experience, it has a more significant impact on what level they achieve than anything else, including their background or previous achievements.[5] Most children learn more deeply when they can apply their knowledge to real problems and when they take part in projects that require collaboration.[6] [7]

Children usually enjoy creating things and undertaking projects. Projects promote shared experiences and shared learning. They are also a good way to enhance interpersonal skills, such as negotiating and explaining feelings. Simple examples of practical projects, depending on the age and ability of the child, could include: brainstorming ideas for a wildlife-friendly garden, learning how to organise and run a sports team, looking after a pet, helping to design a house or creating a healthy meal plan for a week.

By working on projects, children show an increase in the ability to define problems[8] and by experience they also learn how to plan a project.[9]

Sharing experiences and teamwork

Sharing experiences with others can have beneficial effects on us. A shared experience can help to form and strengthen teams and create team bonding, hence the popular team-building days that many companies engage in. These team days are aimed at highlighting different aspects of teamwork and involve practical tasks that usually necessitate collaboration.[10]

For children, a task involving each child contributing in a specific area is a good way to ensure that everyone feels a necessary part of the success of the project.

Learning to work in a team with others can also enhance a child's ability to see other points of view.

Teamwork helps me to see other points of view.

A caution

When it comes to sharing, people will react differently. It might be worth making sure that your child realises that not everyone will share and that different children work in different ways. However, this shouldn't put them off from doing what they feel is right.

Troubleshooting

It's all well and good to hear the research, but the reality of helping children to share can be very different! Tantrums and squabbling, even with outbursts of violence, are not uncommon. So how do we try and prevent this?

Little Tim's attempt at sharing

The following scenario has some very common themes that I have often been asked to help unravel. The distress to the parent is uncomfortable to see and thankfully there are ways forward to remove the stress.

Tim's mother, Angela, has invited her friend Sarah and son Rich to come over to her house for coffee. Sarah and Rich arrive and the two boys meet each other. 'Play nicely,' says Angela. Within minutes, the two boys both want the same toy and war breaks out. Little Tim screams at Rich and punches him, and Rich hits back and bursts into tears. Tim then throws a temper tantrum and runs off. The distraught mothers try to calm things down and Tim then attacks his mother Angela.

Angela is mortified and thinks to herself, 'I can't invite people over, because either my son is a sociopath or clearly I am a bad mother.' Angela doesn't know whether to chastise her son or calm him down by consoling him. She also worries about what others will think about her choice of reaction: discipline or console her son. Alternatively, she thinks, 'Perhaps this is all normal, so I will just ignore it or play it down.' Muddled and stressed, she then condemns herself as a bad mother for not knowing what to do. How does she go forward?

As I said, the above scenario is a dramatic variant on a theme, but sadly one that presents frequently. So what can you do practically to prevent the situation or manage it, if it does occur?

Some ideas on prevention and management of conflict

First let's look at the non-negotiables in this situation and how to work with them.

Children don't usually like to share

Children especially don't like to share if they feel they will miss out. The well-known experiment where two children are asked to decide how to share some sweets demonstrates this nicely.[11] One child is given some sweets to share with another child. The first child has the power to decide how many sweets each of them will get. When this decision is made, the second child has the right to decide if this is reasonable. They can then either accept the offer or reject it, in which case neither child receives any sweets. If the first child doesn't give equal amounts to both of them, the second child almost invariably rejects the offer and would rather have no sweets than see the first child get more.

This sense of fairness and sharing is very strongly in-built into our Chimp circuits and is demonstrated in experiments with primates.[12] [13] [14] The older we get, the better we usually manage this. A young child has little chance of managing this in-built mechanism. Therefore, the starting point is accepting this and knowing that there is nothing wrong with the child. They are under a powerful in-built influence. The sense of fairness is built on expectations that the Chimp circuits have. The Chimp has a preconceived idea of what *should* happen and then becomes distressed if this is not what occurs. The Chimp does not expect surprises and therefore expects fairness will always happen. The Human circuits, however, recognise that life is not always going to go to plan.

How could we manage this?

I can only offer some ideas, but as always you must decide for yourself how you feel it will work for you and your child. The first offer is to prepare the child before these forces try to kick in. Depending on how able the child is to understand the concept of a Chimp machine, you could try to explain that this is what their Chimp will try and do. The child can then understand that it is not them that is becoming aggressive. This is a really important concept, because young children who are told that they are 'bad' very often find it hard to remove this comment from their minds. The child could be asked to join in with a plan to manage their Chimp, should it try to hijack them when it comes to sharing. What happens if the child is too young? This moves nicely on to a programmed behavioural response.

Instilling behaviours and values

We all can learn from responses from others to our behaviours. Children who struggle to understand concepts or ideas can work well with behaviours. The obvious method is to use the reward of approval.

Most children want to have an adult's approval for what they do. If the child has a clear idea of what it takes to gain that approval then they are more likely to conform to this. Therefore, setting out beforehand a behaviour that will gain your approval makes more desirable behaviours likely to happen. You can think of various ways that you can encourage or reward a desirable behaviour, before the attempt at sharing happens.

Addressing beliefs in the child

Our behaviours are typically based on our beliefs. So, for example, if the child believes that another child might break their toys or damage them, they will still be unlikely to share. Either helping the child to accept that toys do get broken or offering to replace any broken toys could help this belief to settle down. You could, of course, agree with the child to remove any special toys before the visitors arrive.

The child will be functioning in the here and now, which most of us do all day long. Therefore, in this mindset we have a tendency to overreact and not see beyond the immediate situation. We can adjust this reaction by reminding ourselves that every situation is temporary. A child can also be helped to do this by reminding them that their friend is only there for a short time; after this, they will have their toys to themselves.

Again, by discussing with the child any beliefs they might be holding as to why they might not want to share, the beliefs can be addressed and hopefully the child's behaviour will alter.

Prepare yourself

Preparing yourself is probably the most important factor for improving the chances of a good outcome. Remember that there are no magic formulae for good parenting but there are guidelines. Even experts disagree on how to manage difficult situations, so try and work out for yourself what will resonate or work for you. Whatever happens during the day regarding childcare, try not to beat yourself up – it is extremely unhelpful. All you can ever do is your best and keep on learning by experience. Be realistic: just about every parent has experienced their child misbehaving at some time, and particularly in public. Often the misbehaviour feels cringeworthy, embarrassing or humiliating. By talking to other parents, I am sure you will gain some reassurance that they have experienced similar incidents. If you still feel your child is acting in an extreme manner then be proactive in seeking out some professional help.

Parents frequently ask me if they could be 'damaging' their child. 'Damage' is probably not a useful word. We all have an idea of what we mean by damage: some form of long-term problem in the child that has arisen during childhood and was created by a carer or parent.

When psychological harm occurs by a parent or carer it is usually quite dramatic and sustained over a long period of time. Should you feel that you have not created the best atmosphere or not handled things in the best way, then see if you can think of how to go forward rather than looking back. If you think you could have handled things better, reflect on how you could do things differently in the future. If you have been sharp with a child then an apology with an explanation can help a lot. Children who suffer persistent severe adversity, psychologically and physically, at the hands of a carer usually turn this around later in life. Most children learn to accept that adults can be unpredictable, and this ironically can help prepare them for the reality of the outside world. (Note: I am not saying this gives you approval to be unpredictable!)

No matter how you conduct yourself and whatever your relationship with your child is, the most important point is that the child feels loved, supported and valued.

Important point

The best you can offer any child is to love, support and value them unconditionally.

Preparing the child

We have already mentioned discussing beliefs and stating what is considered a helpful behaviour with the child. If you want to establish a helpful behaviour, then practising will go a long way to achieving your aim. Most children enjoy role-play. It can be useful to let the child have a go at practising unhelpful and then helpful behaviours and considering the consequences of both. It might also be useful, during this game, for you the adult to ask the child what you could do to help them to behave well.

It takes time to establish helpful behaviours, so patience is beneficial! Behaviours are best learnt in a few steps, so that the child can follow a routine.

What if the battle still happens?

No matter how much we plan in life, we don't always get things to go our way. Circumstances, unforeseen occurrences and our Chimp's reaction can all sabotage the best plans. Why would it be any different for a child?

It is a natural but usually unhelpful reaction for a child to act emotionally. We can't put plans in place for every eventuality. Therefore, acceptance of the situation and rethinking would help. Remember that the situation will end and is time-limited. When a child acts emotionally, for example, by being aggressive, panicking or overreacting, try not to jump to bizarre conclusions.

If a child is displaying violence, it doesn't mean that they will end up in prison, and neither does it mean they will continue with this into adolescence or adult life. It just means that at this point in time, this is how the child is expressing themselves. Children who scream and roll on the floor are highly unlikely to be doing this at 20 years old. What it would mean is having a discussion with the child about what they are feeling at that moment and what could be the alternative ways of expressing themselves. Each child has to learn from their own reactions but can be helped by an adult.

Seeing a child acting out is likely to make the parent feel uncomfortable. Rather than the parent reacting to these uncomfortable feelings, they could accept them and plan how to use them. In some sense, being a parent has similarities to being a coach in sport. No matter how good the coach is, it is eventually up to the athlete to perform. *Even the most skilled parents can't guarantee a well-behaved child.* Children must be helped to eventually learn how to manage themselves.

If you have already formed and agreed a plan with the child on what will happen if the child's Chimp hijacks them, then this plan can be carried out. It is always best to discuss the event when it has ended and after the child has calmed down. They will then be able to review what happened and gain some hope for going forward. In this discussion it will help the child immensely to know that most children have also experienced what they have experienced.

Summary

- Altruism can improve well-being and be part of sharing
- Sharing can improve friendships
- Sharing can implement values
- Practical projects, collaboration and teamwork are based on sharing
- Preparing, discussion and plans can help to prevent and manage conflict

Chapter 16

Habit 10 – doing what you have to do

This chapter addresses how we manage to make ourselves do what we have to do, even if it isn't very pleasant. This is something we could learn early in life, and if we can accept it and get it right, it can make life run a lot more smoothly.

- The untidy bedroom scenarios
- Managing the situation
- What beliefs underpin the feelings?
- The Computer needs input
- Programming in helpful beliefs and behaviours
- Complaining and moaning addressed
- Chimp thinking

The untidy bedroom scenarios

I will start with two scenarios that will be used to demonstrate the basis for developing the habit of getting on with what we have to do, whether we like it or not. The untidy bedroom scenario is so common that finding a child, particularly a teenager, who has a tidy bedroom, is the unusual one!

Lilly the teenager

Picture it: Lilly's bedroom looks as if it's been ransacked. The bedroom becomes the confrontation setting to sit down and discuss things. That is, of course, if you can find somewhere to sit down among the debris.

Here is the scenario that I am frequently told about by a distressed parent. The parent begins, 'All I ask is that she keeps her bedroom tidy. I have explained it is a disgrace and disrespectful to me. I have explained that it is dirty and reflects very poor values from her. I have asked her what she thinks this shows about her. I have asked what she thinks other people would think. I have told her that this is my house and when she gets her own house, she can do what she likes, but not here. I plead, "When you take your clothes off, hang them up in the wardrobe!"', and so the list of comments continues.

Then Lilly replies: 'I just wish they would stop nagging me. I don't have the energy; I am tired all the time. I am so busy I can't get around to it. I don't tell them how to keep their bedroom. Our house is messy and I don't make the mess, so why don't they tidy up after themselves? I can't wait to get out of here. When I have a daughter, I won't nag her – I will let her have her privacy. I do tidy up when I am ready; I just need to be in the right mood. I don't think it's that bad, anyway.'

Kyle the child

Kyle is seven years old and has been playing in his bedroom, which is now in a shambolic state. Despite being asked to tidy up, he has moved two items in thirty minutes. When confronted he rolls on the floor, becomes selectively deaf and refuses to make eye contact. When forced onto his feet, he begins to roam the bedroom, randomly moving items and doing very little. The parent's Chimp begins to surface and loses it: 'Why can't you just be sensible like everyone else?' The child's Chimp retaliates: 'I am doing it, stop shouting at me.'

I am not sure what I am actually learning from all of this!

Managing the situation

Here are some ideas on how you might approach the problem of the untidy bedroom.

Try to be realistic!

Ask yourself how you would expect a typical teenager or child to behave when it comes to being tidy. Most teenagers and children will be at a stage of being untidy and disorganised, but this will improve as they enter adulthood. Research shows that the parent's inability to be realistic in their expectation of a changing adolescent can create problems for the adolescent.[1]

Young people can find it hard to manage many of their feelings. This poor ability to manage emotions can lead to unhelpful behaviours, such as procrastination or avoidance. The problem of untidiness is commonly found in children and young adults, and most people manage to 'grow out' of this, or at least find a balance when it comes to tidiness. So what would be worth considering is why some of us get stuck with being untidy and others get the hang of how to manage their behaviour. If we see it as a learnt behaviour, then we can see being tidy or untidy as just a habit.

Managing feelings

Not getting on with any task that has to be done is usually based on not being able to manage feelings. These feelings are based in the Chimp circuits of the brain and therefore the problem becomes, yet again, a case of learning to recognise interference and then managing the Chimp. Why would we get feelings that prevent us from doing what we know we ought to be doing?

What beliefs underpin the feelings?

What beliefs could be causing the feelings of indifference, agitation, apathy or reluctance to act?

To start with, have we thought through the advantages of getting on with something that we want to do and also the feelings that will continue if we don't act?

It's interesting that, if we were able to sit Lilly and Kyle down and discuss this, we would nearly always find that they would want to have a tidy bedroom. It would be rare to hear someone say, 'I really like living in this mess.' So, have they sat down and thought through why they would like a tidy bedroom, before they attempt to make this happen? A great starting point is to know **what you would like to achieve** before you take on the Chimp.

The Computer needs input

As always, once the Human has decided on what the outcome would ideally be, in order to manage the Chimp we turn to the Computer.

Before we look at the Computer programme that will help us to get started and complete what we want to achieve, it's worth looking at what the Computer will do if it isn't programmed.

If there is no programmed behaviour to tackle the avoidance of getting on with things or the procrastination that prevents us getting started, then either the Chimp will take over or the Computer will revert to unhelpful behaviours.

It's not surprising then that Lilly and Kyle have responses that are unhelpful, defensive and irritating to the parent.

Programming in helpful beliefs and behaviours

Once again, it's helpful to try to programme in helpful beliefs and behaviours during a time when the Chimp isn't in control. So make time to sit and think through the advantages of removing procrastination and avoidance from our behaviour.

How will I feel as soon as I get started?

This has a potential pitfall, and it's a big one! One of the main problems with getting started is that the Chimp sees the task as overwhelming. If there was *one easy step* to do that could be done fairly quickly then the Chimp would have very little resistance to starting. So one of the secrets of programming the Computer is to *make the first step easy*. For tidying the bedroom this could be to just tidy one corner or maybe pick up any clothes. This smaller step will encourage the Chimp to get going, because it is no longer overwhelmed. We also feel encouraged if we can see that a step has been taken and we can celebrate this!

Over the years of working with students, a very common problem that I meet is the student who genuinely wants to study hard but just can't get down to it. The task is seen as too big to take on. By limiting the study time to just 15 minutes and to tackling just one small learning section, most students then get started and focus only on this. Similar small steps usually follow this initial step, which then gets them into a full study pattern.

How will I feel once I have done the task?

By thinking about how you will feel when you get things done, it's easy to see that it will feel like a weight off your mind. So pausing to think about this before getting started will usually help to drive you on. Research shows that this kind of reasoning does not come easily to young children and adolescents. The reasoning appears late in their development.[2][3][4]

Self-image

Most people and most children would describe themselves as being a decent person with a good work ethic. Sadly, as is obvious from life's experiences, many people don't seem to have any insight! We delude ourselves because we want to see ourselves as having the traits we would like to have. If we stop and reflect on the actual behaviours we operate with, it can make us change these behaviours, if they don't reflect what we would like to see in ourselves. So stopping and reflecting on how you see yourself and the reality of a situation can be a good wake-up call to make changes. Children are no different. When I ask a child how they would like to be, up until now I have not had a child that hasn't said something along the lines of, 'I would like to be good.' With assistance, they include things like being hard-working, respectful, pleasing others and so on.

Self-approval makes us feel good, and promoting this by looking at our actual behaviours can help to get things done.

Self-reflection

Work ethic

The idea of looking at work ethic is often overlooked. This forms part of our self-image. Discussing the various aspects of what work ethic means can help people, and children in particular, to challenge their own ideas on how they wish to behave. Work ethic simply could be thought of as being hard-working, contributing to society and being productive.

It involves taking *responsibility* and being *accountable* for your behaviours towards work. It is linked to the concept of *taking pride* in what you do and the *quality* of your work. Work ethic is one aspect of a person's values being demonstrated.

Don't think!

The way the mind works neuroscientifically is that the Human and Chimp slow things down by interpreting and making decisions about situations. The Computer, on the other hand, just gets on with the job. Therefore, if there really isn't any need to analyse or to make decisions, you can learn to refuse to engage in any discussions and block yourself from thinking. When you know what to do and how to do it, then the motto could be, 'No more thinking! Start now!'

Making it pleasant with a link

It's obvious that making a task pleasurable makes doing it a lot easier. Turning a task into a game usually engages children. For adults and children alike, turning the task into a challenge can help to drive us on. Accepting that not everything that has to be done in life is pleasant, and challenging the assumption that it should be, can be sobering. Rewards of praise or sweeteners, such as listening to music while you get on with the work, can help.

Having the same understanding

What we are trying to do in our eyes is help children develop into rounded adults. However, as adults we have differing ideas on what a rounded adult is. We have entered the domain of opinions. So, in our eyes, if we wish to influence a developing child for the better, then we need to help them have the same understanding that we have. This means recognising our own values, where they have come from and what beliefs they are based on.

For example, we might believe that everyone should work and contribute to society. In order to help the child to see our point of view, this needs an explanation and a discussion with them.

If we believe that tidying up after yourself is necessary, then it helps to explain what we see as the consequences, both practical and moral, of doing this and of not doing this.

Learning commitment

Commitment is made regardless of what we feel like. Success can be achieved by committing to doing something without the need for being 'in the right mood'. If we do something based on our feelings, then we may never get things done. Feelings can be helpful, but it helps to recognise when they are holding us back and then to move them to one side. Good feelings and motivation usually follow commitment.

Complaining and moaning addressed

It is natural to complain or moan if something isn't going the way we expect or want it to, but it isn't usually helpful. Forming a habit of always moaning before engaging in any thinking is easy to do and can easily be replaced with a helpful approach to problems.

Rather than rebuke yourself or someone else about moaning, which isn't that helpful in itself to do, first spend time reflecting. A good question worth asking yourself is: 'Is moaning and complaining helping or achieving anything?' If the answer is 'yes' then maybe you could ask, 'Is there a better way of achieving what I want?' If the answer is 'no', then just realising this can help to reshape your habit of dealing with unwelcome situations or setbacks. One good reason to moan is to get things off your chest. Many people find it helpful to have a good moan. Nobody else probably wants to hear the moaning, so it could help to moan to yourself! If you want to moan, a constructive thing can be to set yourself a time limit.

If you don't find moaning and complaining helpful, or you don't want to do this, then what is the alternative? One way to form a new habit is to always try to think of something positive to say about any situation. Usually there are plenty of positive comments that can be made. When you make a positive comment, you have a chance to look for a solution to the negative moan you were about to make.

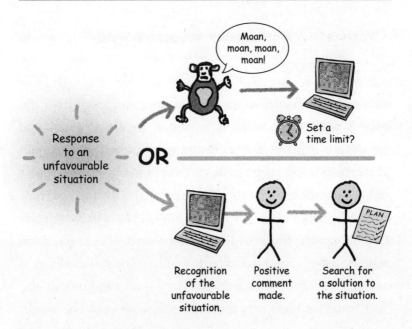

Chimp thinking

Children necessarily think in Chimp mode most of the time in order to protect themselves from danger. However, it can help to discuss things they don't want to do in shades of grey rather than black and white. Children who tell us that they hate school and can't wait to leave rarely have a good comment to make about school life. If you help them to draw up two columns of the good points and the not-so-good points about school, they can begin to appreciate that nearly everything in life has its upside and downside.

Children also move into Chimp mode when they become defiant about not doing something that they don't want to do. Sometimes they can come up with the answer to the problem if they are asked for their opinion on how to solve things. The next scenario demonstrates this.

Years ago, I worked with a young athlete who would throw tantrums whenever they couldn't do what they wanted or were asked to do things that they didn't want to do. It was a very frustrating situation. I sat down with the athlete when they were in a better frame of mind and simply asked them: 'What should we do when you play up and refuse to engage sensibly?' They thought for a while, and then smiled, and said: 'The thing that will stop me from being difficult is if you tell me to stop being a baby. I really hate being told that.' So I wrote on a card the phrase 'Stop being a baby'. The next time the athlete began to throw a tantrum, the card was held up. They took one look at the card, burst into laughter and cooperated! It might be worth asking a child who is prone to difficult behaviour, what they think should happen.

Summary

- Having realistic expectations of children will help
- Beliefs usually underpin feelings
- The Computer needs input if it is to help us
- Discussion on self-image and work ethic can bring change
- Try and get the child and yourself to have the same understanding of situations, so that you are working from the same basis
- Removing the habit of moaning calls for a new approach

Chapter 17

Final thoughts

I hope you have enjoyed reading this book and that it has given you some ideas, encouragement and inspiration. While writing it, I appreciate that there is a risk of me appearing to be instructing rather than advising. Please remember that only you can decide what is best for you and for any children that you are caring for. Any ideas or information that resonates with you, try and use, but don't be afraid to throw out those ideas or thoughts that don't resonate. All of us who work in the field of helping others, whatever our background, are trying to share knowledge and experience. If you do find yourself struggling, I would encourage you to seek professional help. There are a lot of professionals, such as psychologists, psychiatrists, therapists, social workers, counsellors and family doctors who can help, apart from family and friends.

If you are going it alone, try to be realistic about managing yourself or your child. Just like adults, habits form slowly in children and constant repetition and encouragement are needed. Patience is a must! Along with the other ten habits detailed here, we could have added the skill or habit of listening. Teaching a child to be able to listen to what is being said is not as easy as it sounds. Again, patient repetition is very helpful.

Whatever you do, and however you nurture a child, the

most important factor remains; children gain stability by being *loved and respected*... and we are no different as adults!

Love and treat yourself with respect. I wish you every success.

Notes

Part 1: Setting the Scene

Introduction

1.   Bornstein, M.H., et al. (2010). *Lifespan Development: Infancy Through Adulthood*, California, Cengage Learning.

Encouragement for the reader

1.   Oomen, C.A., et al. (2010). 'Severe early life stress hampers spatial learning and neurogenesis, but improves hippocampal synaptic plasticity and emotional learning under high-stress conditions in adulthood.' *Journal of Neuroscience* 30(19): 6635–6645.

2.   Hart, H. and Rubia, K. (2012). 'Neuroimaging of child abuse: a critical review.' *Frontiers in Human Neuroscience* 6(52): 1–24.

3.   Brief summary of research, including references (1) and (2). Rejection by parents or peers: When children are developing, two particular regions of the brain work together to manage some aspects of emotional stability. The amygdala is a very reactive structure that evokes strong emotion. The ventromedial prefrontal cortex (VMPFC) has many functions but one of them is to calm the amygdala down. Children who have caring and warm parents show a good development of the VMPFC. This means that when they become stressed the amygdala is calmed down by the developed VMPFC. Sadly, children who do not have caring parents, or who have experienced rejection by their parents, or have parental separation, show an under-developed VMPFC. This means that it cannot calm the amygdala down when the child becomes stressed. Research shows that later in life, this results in these

children being very sensitised to rejection by parents and peers. They show an increased fear response to rejection.

4. Drew, L.M., et al. (1998). 'Grandparenting and its relationship to parenting.' *Clinical Child Psychology and Psychiatry* 3(3): 465–480.

5. Wyman, P.A., et al. (1999). 'Caregiving and developmental factors differentiating young at-risk urban children showing resilient versus stress-affected outcomes: A Replication and Extension.' *Child Development* 70(3): 645–659.

Part 2: Some Basic Neuroscience

Chapter 1: The simplified neuroscience of the mind

1. Rolls, E.T. and Grabenhorst, F. (2008). The orbitofrontal cortex and beyond: From affect to decision-making. *Progress in Neurobiology* 86: 216–244.

2. Peters, S. (2012). *The Chimp Paradox: The Mind Management Programme to Help You Achieve Success, Confidence, and Happiness*. London, Vermilion.

3. Tsujimoto, S. (2008). 'The Prefrontal Cortex: Functional Neural Development During Early Childhood.' *Neuroscientist* 14(4): 345–358.

4. Cameron, O.G. (2009). 'Visceral brain–body information transfer.' *NeuroImage* 47(3): 787–794.

5. Sokolowski, K., and Corbin, J.G. (2012). 'Wired for behaviors: from development to function of innate limbic system circuitry.' *Frontiers in Molecular Neuroscience* 5 (55): 1–15.

6. Euston, D.R., et al. (2012). 'The role of medial prefrontal cortex in memory and decision making.' *Neuron* 76(6): 1057–1070.

7. Phelps, E.A. (2004). 'Human emotion and memory: Interactions of the amygdala and hippocampal complex.' *Current Opinion in Neurobiology* 14(2): 198–202.

8.   Tovote, P., et al. (2015). 'Neuronal circuits for fear and anxiety.' *Nature Reviews Neuroscience* 16(6): 317–331.

9.   Zander, T., et al. (2016). 'Intuitive decision making as a gradual process: investigating semantic intuition-based and priming-based decisions with fMRI.' *Brain Behaviour* 6(1): 1–22.

10.   A simple explanation of the above references (7), (8), and (9) is as follows. One main area that gets talked a lot about is the amygdala. The amygdala can be thought of as a battery of energy with our main survival defence process of flight, fight or freeze (Tovote et al, 2015). It also monitors many of our drives, such as those for food and security. However, it doesn't really think as such. It reacts to situations and stimuli but it doesn't analyse them. It does store emotional memory and therefore the amygdala is partly Chimp and partly Computer. The survival part of the brain, that does the analysing for it, is the orbitofrontal cortex (part of the Chimp). This area leads on the interpretation of what is going on by using feelings and intuition (Zander, 2015). It calls on other areas to help it with this. So what we have is an emotionally based interpreting and thinking brain, the orbito frontal cortex, connected to a very powerful reactive area, the amygdala. With other structures, these form a genetically based thinking system. Children operate from this system most of the time. In order that the child remembers their experiences, the brain has a memory bank. However, the memory bank for this system is also emotionally based. It records feelings and emotions from experiences but NOT facts. This emotional memory is stored in different parts of the brain but significantly it is stored in the amygdala (Phelps, 2004). The emotional memory system is very fast to act.

    If the brain had no further areas or systems then these two systems, Chimp and Computer, could run the child's life. However, it would not recall facts nor would it possess logic or reasoning. In fact, many functions would not be present.

11.   Duvernoy, H.M. (2005). *The Human Hippocampus: Functional Anatomy, Vascularization and Serial Sections with MRI*. New York, Springer.

12. Bohbot, V., et al. (2015). 'Role of the parahippocampal cortex in memory for the configuration but not the identity of objects: converging evidence from patients with selective thermal lesions and fMRI.' *Frontiers in Molecular Neuroscience* 9(431): 1–17.

13. Fischetti, M. (2011). 'Computers versus Brains.' from https://www.scientificamerican.com/article/computers-vs-brains/

Chapter 2: The developing mind

1. Somerville, L.H. (2016). 'Searching for signatures of brain maturity: What are we searching for?' *Neuron* 92(6): 1164–1167.

2. Johnson, S.B., et al. (2009). 'Adolescent maturity and the brain: The promise and pitfalls of neuroscience research in adolescent health policy.' *Journal of Adolescent Health* 45(3): 216–221.

3. Waters, E. and Cummings, E.M. (2000). 'A Secure Base from Which to Explore Close Relationships.' *Child Development* 71 (1): 164–172.

4. McElhaney, K.B. et al. (2009). *Attachment and Autonomy During Adolescence*. New Jersey, John Wiley & Sons Inc.

5. Wellman, H.M. (1990). *The Child's Theory of Mind*. Cambridge, MIT Press.

6. Perner, J. (1991). *Understanding the Representational Mind*. Cambridge, MIT Press.

7. Roxo, M., et al. (2011). 'The limbic system conception and its historical evolution.' *Scientific World Journal* 11: 2428–2441.

8. Reisberg D., and Heuer, F. (1992). 'Remembering the details of emotional events' in In E. Winograd & U. Neisser (eds.), *Emory symposia in cognition, 4. Affect and accuracy in recall: Studies of "flashbulb" memories* (pp. 162-190). New York, Cambridge University Press.

9. Waring, J. and Kensinger, E.A. (2011). 'How emotion leads to selective memory: neuroimaging evidence.' *Neuropsychologia* 49(7): 1831–1842.

Chapter 3: The neuroscience of the developing mind

1. Kendler, K.S. et al. (1992). 'Major depression and generalized anxiety disorder. Same genes, (partly) different environments?' *Archives of General Psychiatry* 49(9): 716–722.

2. Arch, J.J. et al. (2013). 'Randomized clinical trial of adapted mindfulness-based stress reduction versus group cognitive behavioral therapy for heterogeneous anxiety disorders.' *Behaviour Research and Therapy* 51(4-5): 185–196.

3. Goldin, P.R., and Gross, J.J. (2010). 'Effects of mindfulness-based stress reduction (MBSR) on emotion regulation in social anxiety disorder.' *Emotion* 10(1): 83–91.

4. Davies, G., et al. (2011). 'Genome-wide association studies establish that human intelligence is highly heritable and polygenic.' *Molecular Psychiatry* 16(10): 996–1005.

5. Makharia, A., et al. (2016). 'Effect of environmental factors on intelligence quotient of children.' *Industrial Psychology* 52(16): 189–194.

6. Humphrey, T. and Hooker, D. (1959). 'Double simultaneous stimulation of human fetuses and the anatomical patterns underlying the reflexes elicited.' *Journal of Comparative Neurology* 112(1959): 75–102.

7. Piontelli, A., et al. (1997). 'Patterns of evoked behaviour in twin pregnancies during the first 22 weeks of gestation.' *Early Human Development* 50: 39–45.

8. Marx, V., and Nagy, E. (2017). 'Fetal behavioral responses to the touch of the mother's abdomen: A frame-by-frame analysis.' *Infant Behavior & Development* 47: 83–91.

9. Blaas, H.G., et al. (1998). 'The growth of the human embryo. A longitudinal biometric assessment from 7 to 12 weeks of gestation.' *Ultrasound in Obstetrics and Gynecology* 12(5): 346–354.

10. DeCasper, A. J., and Spence, M.J. (1986). 'Prenatal maternal speech influences newborns' perception of speech sound.' *Infant Behavior & Development* 9(2): 133–150.

11. DiPietro, J.A., et al. (1996). 'Fetal antecedents of infant temperament.' *Child Development* 67(5): 2568–2583.

12. Bao, A.M., and Swaab, D.F. (2011). 'Sexual differentiation of the human brain: Relation to gender identity, sexual orientation and neuropsychiatric disorders.' *Frontiers in Neuroendocrinology* 32(2): 214–226.

13. Blazer, D.G., and Hybels, C. (2005). 'Origins of depression in later life.' *Psychological Medicine* 35(9): 1241–1252.

14. Hoehl, S., et al. (2017). '"Itsy Bitsy Spider": Infants react with increased arousal to spiders and snakes.' *Frontiers in Psychology* 8 (1710): 1–8.

15. LoBue, V. and DeLoache, J.S. (2010). 'Superior detection of threat-relevant stimuli in infancy.' *Developmental Science.* 13(1): 221–228.

16. Waters, E., and Cummings, E.M. (2000). 'A secure base from which to explore close relationships.' *Child Development* 71(1): 164–172.

17. Al Odhayani, A., et al. (2013). 'Behavioural consequences of child abuse.' *Canadian Family Physician* 59(8): 831–836.

18. Bandura, A. (1977). *Social Learning Theory*. Englewood Cliffs, NJ, Prentice Hall.

19. Bandura, A. (1986). *Social Foundations of Thought and Action: A Social Cognitive Theory*. Englewood Cliffs, NJ, Prentice-Hall, Inc.

20. Bandura, A., et al. (1961). 'Transmission of aggression through imitation of aggressive models.' *Journal of Abnormal and Social Psychology* 63(3): 575–582.

21. Zimmerman, M.A., et al. (1994). 'Resiliency research: Implications for schools and policy.' *Society for Research in Child Development* 8(4): 1–19.

22. Reiss, A., Abrams, M., Singer, H., Ross, J. and Denckla, M. (1996). 'Brain development, gender and IQ in children: A volumetric imaging study.' *Brain* 119(5): 1763–1774.

23. Iwasaki, N., et al. (1997). 'Volumetric quantification of brain development using MRI.' *Neuroradiology* 39(12): 841–846.

24. Courchesne, E. et al (2000). 'Normal brain development and aging: quantitative analysis at in vivo MR imaging in healthy volunteers.' *Radiology* 216(3): 672–682.

25. Dehay, C. and Kennedy, D. (2007). 'Cell-cycle control and cortical development.' *Nature Reviews Neuroscience* 8: 438–450.

26. Paus, T., et al. (2001). 'Maturation of white matter in the human brain: a review of magnetic resonance studies.' *Brain Research Bulletin* 54(3): 255–266.

27. Kennedy, D., et al. (2002). 'Basic principles of MRI and morphometry studies of human brain development.' *Developmental Science* 5(3): 268–278.

28. Lenroot, R.K., and Giedd, J.N. (2006). 'Brain development in children and adolescents: insights from anatomical magnetic resonance imaging.' *Neuroscience & Biobehavioral Reviews* 30(6): 718–729.

29. Thompson, P.M., et al. (2000). 'Growth patterns in the developing brain detected by using continuum mechanical tensor maps.' *Nature* 404(6774): 190–193.

30. Johnson, S.B., et al. (2009). 'Adolescent maturity and the brain: The promise and pitfalls of neuroscience research in adolescent health policy.' *Journal of Adolescent Health* 45(3): 216–221.

31. Dosenbach, N.U. et al. (2010). 'Prediction of individual brain maturity using fMRI.' *Science* 329(5997): 1358–1361.

32. Bar-on, M.E. (2001). 'Media violence: Report of the Committee on Public Education.' *Pediatrics* 108(5): 1222–1226.

33. Sharon, T. and Woolley, J.D. (2004). 'Do monsters dream? Young children's understanding of the fantasy/reality distinction.' *British Journal of Developmental Psychology* 22: 293–310.

34. Bowlby, J. (1969). *Attachment and Loss, Vol 1: Attachment.* London, Hogarth Press.

35. Bowlby, J. (1988). *A Secure Base: Clinical Applications of Attachment Theory.* London, Routledge.

36. World Health Organisation (2004). 'The importance of caregiver–child interactions for the survival and healthy development of young children.'

37. Silverstein, L.B., and Auerbach, C.F. (1999). 'Deconstructing the essential father.' *American Psychologist* 54(6): 397–407.

38. Whiteside, M.F. and Becker, B.J. (2000). 'Parental factors and the young child's postdivorce adjustment: a meta-analysis with implications for parenting arrangements.' *Journal of Family Psychology* 14(1): 5–26.

39. Morris, A.S., et al. (2007). 'The role of the family context in the development of emotion regulation.' *Social Development* (Oxford, England) 16(2): 361–388.

40. Goldberg, S., et al. (2013). *Attachment Theory: Social, Developmental, and Clinical Perspectives.* Oxon, Routledge.

41. Avants, B.B., et al. (2015). 'Relation of childhood home environment to cortical thickness in late adolescence: Specificity of experience and timing.' *PLoS ONE* 10(10): 1–10.

42. Rao, H., et al. (2010). 'Early parental care is important for hippocampal maturation: Evidence from brain morphology in humans.' *NeuroImage* 49(1): 1144–1150.

43. Koluchova, J. (1972). 'Severe deprivation in twins: A case study.' *Journal of Child Psychology and Psychiatry* 13: 107–114.

44. Koluchova, J. (1991). 'Severely deprived twins after 22 years of observation.' *Studia Psychologica* 33: 23–28.

45. Curtiss, S. (1977). *Genie: A Psycholinguistic Study of a Modern-day 'Wild Child'*. New York, Academic Press.

46. Spelke, E. (1999). 'Save Mozart for later.' *Nature* 401(6754): 643–644.

47. Kohlberg, L. (1968). 'The child as a moral philosopher.' *Psychology Today* 2(4): 24–30.

Chapter 4: How we make sense of experiences

1. Maag, J.W. (2001). 'Rewarded by punishment: reflections on the disuse of positive reinforcement in schools.' *Exceptional Children* 67(2): 173–186 .

2. Maag, J.W. (1997). *Parenting without punishment: Making problem behaviour work for you*. Philadelphia, The Charles Press.

3. Deci, E.L., Koestner, R., & Ryan, R.M. (1999). 'A meta-analytic review of experiments examining the effects of extrinsic rewards on intrinsic motivation.' *Psychological Bulletin* 125(6): 627–668.

4. Filcheck, H.A., & McNeil, C.B. (2004). 'The use of token economies in preschool classrooms: Practical and philosophical concerns.' *Journal of Early and Intensive Behavior Intervention* 1(1): 94–104.

5. Skinner, B.F. (1953). *Science and Human Behavior*. New York, MacMillan.

6. Bijou, S. (1957). 'Patterns of reinforcement and resistance to extinction in young children.' *Child Development* 28(1): 47–54.

7. Freud, S. (1913). *The Interpretation of Dreams*. New York, Macmillan.

8. Brooker, R.J. et al. (2013). 'The development of stranger fear in infancy and toddlerhood: normative development, individual differences, antecedents, and outcomes.' *Developmental Science* 16(6): 864–878.

9. Field, T. (2008). *Problems in Infancy*. New Jersey, John Wiley & Sons.

Part 3: Ten Habits and Related Themes

1. Smith, K.S. and Graybiel, A.M. (2016). 'Habit formation.' *Dialogues in Clinical Neuroscience* 18(1): 33–43.

2. Yin, H.H. and Knowlton, B.J. (2006). 'The role of the basal ganglia in habit formation.' *Nature Reviews Neuroscience* 7(6): 464–476.

3. Lally, P., et al. (2010). 'How are habits formed: Modelling habit formation in the real world.' *European Journal of Social Psychology* 40(6): 998–1009.

4. Lally, P., et al. (2011). 'Experiences of habit formation: A qualitative study.' *Psychology, Health & Medicine* 16(4): 484–489.

5. Smith, K S. and Graybiel, A.M. (2013). 'A dual operator view of habitual behavior reflecting cortical and striatal dynamics.' *Neuron* 79(2): 361–374.

Chapter 5: Habit 1 – smiling

1. Kraft, T.L., & Pressman, S.D. (2012). 'Grin and bear it: The influence of manipulated facial expression on the stress response.' *Psychological Science* 23: 1372–1378.

2. Strack, F., Martin, L. & Stepper, S. (1988). 'Inhibiting and facilitating conditions of the human smile: A nonobtrusive test

of the facial feedback hypothesis.' *Journal of Personality and Social Psychology* 54: 768–777.

3. Soussignan, R. (2002). 'Duchenne smile, emotional experience and autonomic reactivity: A test of the facial feedback hypothesis.' *Emotion* 2: 52–74.

4. Larsen, R.J., Kasimatis, M., & Frey, K. (1992) 'Facilitating the furrowed brow: An unobtrusive test of the facial feedback hypothesis applied to unpleasant affect.' *Cognition and Emotion* 6: 321–338.

5. Guéguen, N. (2003). 'The effect of smiling on helping behavior: Smiling and good Samaritan behavior.' *Communication Reports* 16: 133–140.

6. Bai, S., Repetti, R.L., & Sperling, J.B. (2016). 'Children's expressions of positive emotion are sustained by smiling, touching, and playing with parents and siblings: A naturalistic observational study of family life.' *Developmental Psychology* 52(1): 88–101.

7. Frith, C. (2009). 'Role of facial expressions in social interactions.' *Philosophical Transactions of the Royal Society B: Biological Sciences* 364(1535): 3453–3458.

8. Somerville, L.H., et al. (2011). 'Behavioral and neural representation of emotional facial expressions across the lifespan.' *Developmental Neuropsychology* 36(4): 408–428.

9. Hennenlotter, A., Dresel, C., Castrop, F., Wohlschläger, A.M., & Haslinger, B. (2009). 'The link between facial feedback and neural activity within central circuitries of emotion: New insights from botulinum toxin-induced denervation of frown muscles.' *Cerebral Cortex* 19(3): 537–542.

10. Lau, S. (1982). 'The effect of smiling on person perception.' *Journal of Social Psychology* 117: 63–67.

Chapter 6: Habit 2 – saying sorry

1. Strang, S., Utikal, V., Fischbacher, U., Weber, B., & Falk, A. (2014). 'Neural correlates of receiving an apology and active forgiveness: An fMRI Study.' *PLoS ONE* 9(2): e87654. http://doi.org/10.1371/journal.pone.0087654

2. Anderson, J.C., Linden, W., & Habra, M.E. (2006). 'Influence of apologies and trait hostility on recovery from anger.' *Journal of Behavioural Medicine* 29(4): 347–58.

3. McCullough, M.E., Pedersen, E.J., Tabak, B.A., & Carter, E.C. (2014). 'Conciliatory gestures promote forgiveness and reduce anger in humans.' *Proceedings of the National Academy of Sciences of the United States of America* 111(30): 11211–11216. http://doi.org/10.1073/pnas.1405072111

4. Jeter, W.K., & Brannon, L.A. (2017). 'I'll Make It Up to You': Examining the effect of apologies on forgiveness.' *Journal of Positive Psychology* 13(6): 1–8.

5. Bentley, J.M. (2015). 'Shifting identification: A theory of apologies and pseudo-apologies.' *Public Relations Review* 41(1): 22–29.

6. Whited, M.C., Wheat, A.L. & Larkin, K.T. (2010). 'The influence of forgiveness and apology on cardiovascular reactivity and recovery in response to mental stress.' *Journal of Behavioral Medicine* 33(4): 293–304.

7. Darby, B.W., & Schlenker, B.R. (1982). 'Children's reactions to apologies.' *Journal of Personality and Social Psychology* 43(4): 742–753.

8. Lazare, A. (2004). *On Apology*. New York, Oxford University Press.

9. Bornstein, B.H., et al. (2002). 'The effects of defendant remorse on mock juror decisions in a malpractice case.' *Behavioral Sciences & the Law* 20(4): 393–409.

10. Hearit, K.M. (2006). *Crisis Management by Apology: Corporate*

Response to Allegations of Wrongdoing. New Jersey, Lawrence Erlbaum.

11. Benoit, W.L. (1995). *Accounts, Excuses and Apologies: A Theory of Image Repair Strategies*. Albany, State University of New York Press.

12. Schmitt, M., et al. (2004). 'Effects of Objective and Subjective Account Components on Forgiving.' *Journal of Social Psychology* 144(5): 465–486.

13. Scher, S.J., & Darley, J.M. (1997). 'How effective are the things people say to apologize? Effects of the realization of the Apology Speech Act.' *Journal of Psycholinguistic Research* 26(1): 127–140.

14. Tavuchis, N. (1991). *Mea Culpa: A Sociology of Apology and Reconciliation*. Stanford, Stanford University Press.

Chapter 7: Understanding and managing mishaps

1. Cairney, J., Veldhuizen, S., & Szatmari, P., (2010). 'Motor coordination and emotional-behavioral problems in children.' *Current Opinion in Psychiatry* 23(4): 324–329.

2. Balconi, M. (2013). 'Dorsolateral prefrontal cortex, working memory and episodic memory processes: insight through transcranial magnetic stimulation techniques.' *Neuroscience Bulletin* 29(3): 381–389.

Chapter 8: Habit 3 – being kind to others

1. Zaki, J., & Mitchell, J.P. (2011). 'Equitable decision making is associated with neural markers of intrinsic value.' *Proceedings of the National Academy of Sciences* 108(49): 19761–19766.

2. Anik, L., et al. (2009). 'Feeling good about giving: The benefits (and costs) of self-interested charitable behavior.' Harvard Business School Marketing Unit Working Paper No. 10-012.

3. Barraza, J.A., et al. (2013). 'Effects of a 10-day oxytocin trial in older adults on health and well-being.' *Experimental and Clinical Psychopharmacology* 21(2): 85–92.

4. Trivers, R.L. (1971). 'The evolution of reciprocal altruism.' *Quarterly Review of Biology* 46(1): 35–57.

5. Fehr, E., & U. Fischbacher U. (2003). 'The nature of human altruism.' *Nature* 425: 785–791.

Chapter 9: Theory of Mind

1. Gershman, S.J., et al. (2016). 'Plans, habits, and theory of mind.' *PLoS ONE* 11(9): 1–24.

2. Perner, J., et al. (1987). 'Three-year-old's difficulty with false belief: The case for conceptual deficit.' *British Journal of Developmental Psychology* 5(2): 125–137.

3. Peterson, C.C., et al. (2012). 'The mind behind the message: advancing theory-of-mind scales for typically developing children, and those with deafness, autism, or Asperger syndrome.' *Child Development* 83(2): 469–485.

4. Gweon, H., et al. (2012). 'Theory of mind performance in children correlates with functional specialization of a brain region for thinking about thoughts.' *Child Development* 83(6): 1853–1868.

5. Leslie, A.M. (1987). 'Pretence and representation: the origins of "theory of mind".' *Psychological Review* 94(4): 412–426.

Chapter 10: Habit 4 – talking about your feelings

1. Lepore, S.J., Ragan, J.D., & Jones, S. (2000). 'Talking facilitates cognitive-emotional processes of adaptation to an acute stressor.' *Journal of Personality and Social Psychology* 78(3): 499–508.

2. Lindquist, K.A., et al. (2015). 'The role of language in emotion: predictions from psychological constructionism.' *Frontiers in Psychology* 1–17.

3. Lutgendorf, S., & Antoni, M. (1999). 'Emotional and cognitive processing in a trauma disclosure paradigm.' *Cognitive Therapy and Research* 23(4): 423–440.

Chapter 11: Habit 5 – asking for help

1. Metcalfe, J. (2017). 'Learning from errors.' *Annual Review of Psychology* 68(1): 465–489.

2. Schroder, H.S., et al. (2017). 'Neural evidence for enhanced attention to mistakes among school-aged children with a growth mindset.' *Developmental Cognitive Neuroscience* 24: 42–50.

3. Hays, M.J., et al. (2013). 'When and why a failed test potentiates the effectiveness of subsequent study.' *Journal of Experimental Psychology: Learning, Memory, and Cognition* 39: 290–296.

4. Richland, L.E., et al. (2009). 'The pretesting effect: Do unsuccessful retrieval attempts enhance learning?' *Journal of Experimental Psychology: Applied* 15(3): 243–257.

5. Kornell, N., et al. (2009). 'Unsuccessful retrieval attempts enhance subsequent learning.' *Journal of Experimental Psychology: Applied Learning, Memory, and Cognition* 35(4): 989–998.

6. Wilhelm, J.D., & Wilhelm, P.J. (2010). 'Inquiring minds learn to read, write, and think: reaching all learners through inquiry.' *Middle School Journal* 41(5): 39–46.

7. Conezio, K., & French, L. (2002). 'Science in the preschool classroom: Capitalizing on children's fascination with the everyday world to foster language and literacy development.' *Young Children* 57(5): 12–18.

8. Wells, G. (1992). 'Language and the inquiry-oriented curriculum.' *Curriculum Inquiry*. 25(3): 233–269.

9. Applebee, A.N., et al. (2003). 'Discussion-based approaches to developing understanding: Classroom instruction and student performance in middle and high school English.' *American Educational Research Journal* 40(3): 685–730.

10. Stepien, W.J., et al. (1993). 'Problem-based learning for traditional and interdisciplinary classrooms.' *Journal for the Education of the Gifted* 16(4): 338–357.

11. Thomas, J.W. (2000). 'A review of research on project-based learning. California', The Autodesk Foundation. http://www.bie.org/images/uploads/general/9d06758fd346969cb63653d00dca55c0.pdf

12. Boaler, J. (1997). 'Setting, social class and survival of the quickest.' *British Educational Research Journal* 23(5): 575–595.

13. Boaler, J. (1998). 'Open and closed mathematics: Student experiences and understanding.' *Journal for Research in Mathematics Education* 29(1): 41.

14. Meyer, D.K., et al. (1997). 'Challenge in a mathematics classroom: Students' motivation and strategies in project-based learning.' *Elementary School Journal* 97(5): 501–521.

15. Rosenfeld, M., & Rosenfeld, S. (1999). 'Understanding the "Surprises" in PBL: An Exploration into the Learning Styles of Teachers and Their Students'. European Association for Research in Learning and Instruction (EARLI) Sweden.

16. Mantzicopoulos, P., et al. (2008). 'Young children's motivational beliefs about learning science.' *Early Childhood Research Quarterly* 23(3): 378–394.

17. Hamlin, M., & Wisneski, D.B. (2012). 'Supporting the scientific thinking and Inquiry of toddlers and preschoolers through play.' *Young Children* 67(3): 82–88.

18. Smith, M.K., et al. (2009). 'Why peer discussion improves student performance on in-class concept questions.' *Science* 323(5910): 122–124.

19. Vega, V., & Terada, Y. (2012). 'Research supports collaborative learning: Collaborative math and discussion-based English help to promote deeper learning, critical thinking, and community at The College Preparatory School in Oakland, California.' from https://www.edutopia.org/stw-collaborative-learning-research

Chapter 12: Habit 6 – showing good manners

1. Grant A.M., & Gina, F. (2010). 'A little thanks goes a long way: Explaining why gratitude expressions motivate prosocial behaviour.' Journal of Personality and Social Psychology 98(6): 946–55.

2. Sansone. R.A, & Sansone, L.A. (2010). 'Gratitude and well-being: The benefits of appreciation.' *Psychiatry* 7(11): 18–22.

3. Emmons R.A., et al. (2003). 'Counting blessings versus burdens: An experimental investigation of gratitude and subjective well-being in daily life.' *Journal of Personality and Social Psychology* 84(2): 377–89.

4. Lambert, N.M., & Fincham, F.D. (2011). 'Expressing gratitude to a partner leads to more relationship maintenance behavior.' *Emotion* 11(1): 52–60.

5. Giesen, P., et al. (2008). 'Rude or aggressive patient behaviour during out-of-hours GP care: Challenges in communication with patients.' *Patient Education and Counseling* 73(2): 205–208.

6. Brendtro, L.K., & Longhurst, J.E. (2005). 'The resilient brain.' *Reclaiming Children and Youth: The Journal of Strength-based Interventions* 14(1): 52–60.

7. Beer, J.S., et al. (2006). 'Orbitofrontal cortex and social behavior: integrating self-monitoring and emotion-cognition interactions.' *Journal of Cognitive Neuroscience* 18(6): 871–879.

Chapter 13: Habit 7 – trying new things

1. Upton, P. (2011). *Developmental Psychology: Critical Thinking in Psychology*. Exeter, Learning Matters Ltd.

2. O'Connor, B., Wells, C., & Applegate, T. (2015). *Health: You and Your World Volume 1: Brief Edition*: CreateSpace Independent Publishing Platform, 28.

Chapter 14: Habit 8 – Accepting that 'no' means 'no'!

1. Lindquist, K.A., et al. (2015). 'The role of language in emotion: predictions from psychological constructionism.' *Frontiers in Psychology* 6 (444): 1–17.

2. Burke, R.V., et al. (2004). 'Brief report: a "storybook" ending to children's bedtime problems--the use of a rewarding social story to reduce bedtime resistance and frequent night waking.' *Journal of Pediatric Psychology* 29(5): 389–396.

Chapter 15: Habit 9 – learning to share

1. Dunn, E.W., et al. (2008). 'Spending money on others promotes happiness.' *Science* 319(5870): 1687–1688.

2. Eccles, J.S. (1999). 'The development of children ages 6 to 14.' *The Future of Children* 9(2): 30.

3. Niffenegger, J.P., & Wilier, J.P. (1998). 'Friendship behaviors during early childhood and beyond.' *Early Childhood Research Quarterly* 26(2): 95–99.

4. Smith, J., & Prior, M. (1995). 'Temperament and stress resilience in school-age children: a within-families study.' *Journal of the American Academy of Child & Adolescent Psychiatry* 34(2): 168–179.

5. Hohmann, M., & Weikart, D.P. (1995). *Educating Young Children: Active Learning Practices for Preschool and Child Care Programs*. Michigan, High Scope Press.

6. Barron, B., & Darling-Hammond, L. (2008). *Teaching for Meaningful Learning: A Review of Research on Inquiry-Based and Cooperative Learning. Powerful Learning: What We Know About Teaching for Understanding.* San Francisco: John Wiley and Sons Inc.

7. Newmann, F.M., et al. (1995). 'Authentic pedagogy: Standards that boost student performance.' *American Journal of Education* 104(4): 280–312.

8. Gallagher, S.A., et al. (1992). 'The effects of problem-based learning on problem solving.' *Gifted Child Quarterly* 36(4): 195–200.

9. Moore, A., et al. (1996). 'Using problem-based learning to prepare for project-based learning.' Paper presented at the annual meeting of the American Educational Research Association. New York.

10. McEwan, D., et al. (2017). 'The effectiveness of teamwork training on teamwork behaviors and team performance: A systematic review and meta-analysis of controlled interventions.' *PLoS ONE* 12(1): 1–23.

11. Fehr, E., et al. (2008). 'Egalitarianism in young children.' *Nature* 454(7208): 1079–1083.

12. Hare, B., et al. (2007). 'Tolerance allows bonobos to outperform chimpanzees on a cooperative task.' *Current Biology* 17(7): 619–623.

13. Hare, B., & Kwetuenda, S. (2010). 'Bonobos voluntarily share their own food with others.' *Current Biology* 20(5): R230-R231.

14. Tan, J., & Hare, B.(2013). 'Bonobos share with strangers.' *PLoS ONE* 8(1): 1–11.

Chapter 16: Habit 10 – doing what you have to do

1. Collins, A.W. (1997). 'Relationships and development during adolescence: Interpersonal adaptation to individual change.' *Personal Relationships* 4(1): 1–14.

2. Chugani, H.T., et al. (1987). 'Positron emission tomography study of human brain functional development.' *Annals of Neurology* 22(4): 487–497.

3. Paus, T., et al. (1999). 'Structural maturation of neural pathways in children and adolescents: In vivo study.' *Science* 283(5409): 1908–1911.

4. Sowell, E.R., et al. (1999). 'In vivo evidence for post-adolescent brain maturation in frontal and striatal regions.' *Nature Neuroscience.* 2(10): 859–861.

Extract from
My Hidden Chimp

I hope you have found some of the information and ideas in this book helpful. If you are working with children and would like to go through the ten habits with them, I have also written a children's educational book called *My Hidden Chimp* specifically for this purpose. It begins with some basic neuroscience, before covering the ten habits and concluding with a summary – and it also contains activities that children can complete to help them understand the theory.

Some children might be able to work through the book on their own, but I think it would work best if an adult explores the topics and works through the book with them.

Here's an extract from the book to show how it works.

4

Talking about your feelings

Talking about your feelings

Talking about your feelings

Let's look at my friend Chen who shares his feelings with his Auntie Lin.

Chen is feeling frustrated because things have not been going the way he wanted them to. He is upset.

He talks with his Auntie Lin and tells her what has been happening and how he has been feeling.

I am upset!

Please tell me.

Lin listens and Chen feels better because someone has understood how he feels.

Chen thanks his auntie.

I feel better.

I am listening and I understand.

Thank you.

Talking about your feelings

Sometimes my Chimp
is super excited and happy.
I like to share the excitement
with my friends.

Sharing how excited I feel makes it even better.

My Chimp Banana-head got over excited, so I had to tell her to calm down!

I am so excited I am going to explode.

It's great to be excited but don't get silly!

I will dance instead.

It's great to see Banana-head so excited, but you are right she needs to calm down.

Important point:
Sometimes your Chimp needs to let out its excitement first before it can listen.

Talking about your feelings

I decided to talk to someone who cares about me.

Talking about your feelings

Important point:
Sometimes it helps to talk about the same thing more than once.

Index